POLITICS REIMAGINED

An Exploration of Politics Without Politicians

POLITICS REIMAGINED

An Exploration of Politics Without Politicians

**Major General Anil Sengar (Retd) &
Captain Sanjay Gahlot, IRS (Retd)**

THE BROWSER

Title: Politics Reimagined:
An Exploration of Politics Without Politicians
Authors: Major General Anil Sengar (Retd) &
Captain Sanjay Gahlot, IRS (Retd)

ISBN: 978-93-49042-29-2

Published by:
JGS Enterprises Pvt Ltd
Imprint: The Browser

Publisher's Address:
SCO 14-15, FF, Sector 8-C, Chandigarh 160 009

Website: thebrowser.org
Email: service@thebrowser.org

Printed in India

© Layout and Cover Design by 99 beagles
99beagles.com

THE BROWSER

Publishers & Booksellers

Politics is too serious a matter to be left to the politicians.

—Charles de Gaulle

Dedicated to the gullible voter who naively trusts the politicians every five years, with the elusive hope that it would be different this time around.... It rarely is!

And

The warriors who selflessly and relentlessly strive to fight the political malaise at great cost to themselves.

Contents

Part V: The Future of Politics Without Politicians

Part VI: Stop Press

Part VII: Conclusion

Acknowledgement

Politics Reimagined is the product of intense reflection, rigorous dialogue, and a deep concern for the state of our world. This book emerges from a critical examination of political dynamics in India and globally—an exploration that lays bare the erosion of public trust in politicians, the paralysis of democratic institutions, and the moral decay afflicting many centres of power.

As we write, more than 68 nations are in active conflict, others teeter on the brink of collapse, and existential threats—from nuclear escalation to climate catastrophe—loom large. These grim realities formed the crucible in which this work was forged.

We wish to acknowledge the often-troubling contributions of international political actors, whose ineptitude, opportunism, and cynicism have served as both the cautionary tales and the intellectual provocation behind this book. Their failures inspired us to imagine politics differently.

We are grateful to our peers, mentors, and interlocutors who challenged and enriched our thinking. The foundational ideas of this book were shaped through discussions between us, and expanded through the lens of formal political theory studied during the Master's in Political Science by Captain Sanjay

Gahlot and our M.Phil. programme in the Indian Institute of Public Administration, New Delhi. We thank our professors and academic institutions for nurturing critical inquiry, even when it led to uncomfortable questions.

We are not political scientists, but as discerning citizens, we see the need for transformation. With both the co-authors coming from a military background, our upbringing in the highest values of integrity, selfless service, and the nation first helped us see clearly what is lacking and what needs to be fixed in the political discourse.

Major General Anil Sengar has conceptualised cartoons in the book, and illustrations done by Captain Sanjay Gahlot.

Finally, to the countless unnamed citizens, activists, and thinkers across the globe who continue to believe in justice, representation, and collective dignity—this book is, in spirit, for you.

Foreword

◆◆◆

Welcome to Politics Reimagined. As we write this book, the world stands engulfed in crisis—wars rage across continents, and numerous nations teeter on the edge of collapse. Who, if not our elected leaders, are responsible for leading us into this chaos? Meanwhile, the gravest threat to humanity—climate change—is either dismissed outright or met with empty declarations. The critical 1.5°C threshold has already been crossed, and the path ahead points unmistakably toward catastrophe.

Politics refers to the processes, activities, and institutions through which power and resources are distributed, and decisions are made within a group, society, or state. It involves the negotiation of interests, the exercise of authority, the formulation and implementation of public policy, and the mechanisms of governance in the best interest of all people. People who are charged with this responsibility are the elected representatives of the people, called politicians.

When we think of governance, politics and politicians often appear as conjoined twins—inseparable and uncomfortably entangled. Like such twins, their existence together can be burdensome and disruptive, with one often dragging the other down. But imagine a successful surgery that separates them. Freed from their mutual dependence, each can thrive and fulfil its true potential.

Across the globe, the words *politics* and *politicians* no longer inspire confidence. They've become symbols of mistrust, cynicism, corruption, division, and disappointment. But what if we could perform an intellectual surgery—a deliberate act of reimagining politics to separate the essence of politics from the individuals who have come to represent it?

What might emerge is a vision of *politics without politicians*—a redefined, revitalised space for civic engagement, public decision-making, and collective progress, free from the baggage of entrenched interests, partisanship, and personal ambition of the elected representatives. This could ensure that the interests of the people are best addressed.

What are the implications of politics without politicians, and how will the idea work? Do we really need those guys, after all? It is a daring exploration into the possibility of a political landscape devoid of its traditional protagonists. This book invites you on an intellectual journey, questioning the foundational need for politicians in an era where direct democracy is not only possible but perhaps preferable.

In our quest to reimagine governance, we draw on historical precedents, from the direct civic engagements of ancient Athens to the potential of modern technologies like blockchain, which promise transparency and direct public participation in governmental decision-making. By tracing the annals of democracy, this book lays bare the critical assessments of political structures that have often failed to encapsulate the will of the people they serve.

Throughout these pages, you will encounter a vivid tapestry of global and historical contexts that underscore a persistent theme: the contentious and often destructive role of politicians. From the perpetual conflicts influenced by political decisions, such as the numerous wars involving the United States, to the stark inequities and ironies within Indian democracy, the narrative builds a compelling case for a major overhaul of our political systems.

Politics Reimagined: An Exploration of Politics Without Politicians critically examines the paradoxes that plague democracies, where leaders with minimal qualifications or dubious reputations wield significant power, and where a select few dictate policies that shape millions of lives. The discussion extends to the societal implications of these governance models, highlighting the pressing issues of caste discrimination, poverty, and gross inequalities that persist under the watch of traditional political mechanisms.

The barcode of this book can be represented by three examples that cry loudly for the need for direct public participation in matters that affect people.

The first is abortion, where for centuries the Church, far separated from the responsibility of familyhood, had a major say in framing the abortion policies. Similarly, parliaments with minuscule representation of women decide the fate of women on issues that affect only women.

The second, relating especially to India, is the 'Triple Talaq' issue, where a Muslim husband could divorce his wife by repeating 'Talaq' (meaning divorce) three times. The divorce could be affected by the husband by sending such a message on WhatsApp. Ever heard of better exploitation of technology anywhere for perpetuating gross injustice? The Indian government criminalised this practice, restoring dignity to Muslim women. It was the clerics legislating the righteousness of this practice on religious grounds, with women having little say on such an important issue impacting their lives.

The third famous case that deserves a mention is that of the divorced 60-year-old Muslim woman, Shah Bano, where a Supreme Court ruling on the provision of maintenance to her under the provisions of Section 125 of the IPC was mostly undone by the government of the day for political expediency. The Parliament enacted the Muslim Women (Protection of Rights on Divorce) Act, 1986, which restricted the maintenance to the period of Iddah by a one-time settlement, clearly a vague provision.

When this act was enacted, the women's representation in the Lok Sabha was five per cent out of 544 and in the Rajya Sabha was 5.2 per cent out of 250 seats, effectively making them inconsequential. Yet again, a decision that severely impacts women was taken by a male-dominated parliament in a country dominated by a patriarchal mindset.

In the three cases cited above, isn't there a case for direct public participation and a referendum seeking the voice of the affected section of the people?

This foreword sets the stage for a deeper investigation into how direct democracy could rectify these long-standing issues by eliminating or at least downsizing the role of the middleman—the politician. By advocating for a system where the general populace is directly involved in the legislative process, the book proposes not just a shift in how decisions are made but a transformation in who gets to make them.

We were nearing completion of this book when the 2024 United States (US) elections delivered the return of Donald Trump for a second term. The early months of *Trump 2.0* have been marked by a distinctly personal, transactional style of politics that shook the world. Every country has the right to protect its national interest, but his 'America First' rhetoric continues to define a sceptical stance toward supranationalism, traditional alliances, global institutions, and economic order.

The important issue in the context of this book is that a single, democratically elected leader can completely reverse a country's policy, underscoring the urgency of the ideas we explore in this book, the concept of *politics without politicians*, and the principles of institutional accountability. We delve into the implications of *Trump 2.0* in Chapter XV: *The Second Coming of Donald Trump: A Domino Moment for Global Democracy*.

As you read through the book, prepare to challenge your perceptions of political necessity and efficacy. *Politics Reimagined* offers a blend of rigorous analysis, historical insights, and forward-thinking proposals aimed at redefining the essence of governance. It is a call to action for those who envision a democratic process that genuinely reflects the will and welfare of the people.

Let this exploration begin, not just as a critique of the current state of affairs but as a proposition for a new, more engaged form of democracy. This journey promises not only to enlighten but also to inspire action towards realising a political system that truly serves its constituents. As we ponder the role of politicians and the potential for a world without them, may we also consider the greater possibilities that lie in our collective power to shape the future.

Welcome aboard a transformative exploration of what it means to govern and be governed in the true spirit of democracy.

> *The future of humanity is everybody's business. It can't be left to the politicians alone.*

PART I

◆◆◆

Introduction to Politics and Politicians

CHAPTER 1

A Historical Overview of Political Structures: How Politicians Became Central Figures in Governance

Throughout history, societies have organised themselves in various ways to maintain order, allocate resources, and resolve conflicts. Political structures have been fundamental to the evolution of civilisation, guiding how decisions are made and who holds power. The central figure in these structures—the politician—emerged as a result of complex developments in governance, society, and ideology.

This chapter delves into the historical trajectory of political systems, from early tribal councils to modern democracies, exploring how politicians have come to play a central role in governance. The story of politics is not just about the systems but about the people who navigated them, shaped them, and ultimately became the face of governance.

The Tribal Foundations: Elders, Chiefs, and Consensus

In the earliest human societies, governance was based largely on kinship, consensus, and communal decision-making. These tribal societies, often small in number, relied on informal hierarchies where elders or tribal leaders acted as decision-makers, not necessarily as politicians in the modern sense, but more as guides and keepers of wisdom. These figures were selected based on age, experience, or martial prowess and were often seen as natural leaders whose role was to maintain harmony and order within the group.

Political structures during this time were egalitarian, and decision-making was participatory. Everyone had a voice, and leaders did not govern in isolation; rather, they acted on behalf of the collective will. However, the seeds of political centralisation were already being sown, with chiefs and elders often amassing more influence over time, laying the groundwork for future, more formal political structures.

The Rise of Monarchies: The King as the First Politician

As societies expanded and populations grew, governance systems had to evolve. The shift from nomadic tribes to settled agricultural communities around 10,000 BCE brought about the need for more structured political systems. The rise of city-states, such as those in Mesopotamia, Egypt, and the Indus Valley, gave birth to centralised authority in the form of kings and emperors. Monarchs were often viewed as divinely appointed figures, and their power was absolute.

While these rulers were not politicians in the contemporary sense, they laid the foundation for the concept of individual rule. Kings represented their nations on the international stage, formed alliances, and waged wars. Their actions were inherently political, and they often relied on a cadre of advisers, military leaders, and bureaucrats to help govern. These early political actors served as intermediaries between the ruler and the people, slowly forming the class of political figures we recognise today.

Ancient Greece and Rome: The Birth of Political Representation

The true shift toward modern political structures began with the advent of democracy and republicanism in ancient Greece and Rome. In the fifth century BCE Athens, the concept of democracy—rule by the people—was born. Athenian citizens had the right to participate directly in decision-making through the assembly, though this right was limited to free male citizens. The politicians of Athens, such as Pericles, were individuals who could persuade the assembly, present proposals, and represent their fellow citizens. Politics began to shift from being about hereditary rule to a process in which individuals competed for influence.

While the Athenian system's design and implementation diverged significantly from the representative democracy most of us are familiar with today, useful lessons can be derived from its democratic practices.

In contemporary democracies, citizens typically cast their votes for representatives or politicians who, in turn, make decisions on their behalf. These representatives, once elected, have the authority to create, modify, and implement laws, while the common citizen's involvement usually ends at the ballot box until the next election.

In stark contrast, the Athenian model encouraged citizens to be directly involved in the city-state's day-to-day governance. This was a radical departure from other forms of governance of that era, placing the very essence of power into the hands of its citizens.

We will briefly look at some ancient Athenian democratic practices that can be suitably adapted to the modern world.

Ekklesia: Ekklesia, or Assembly, was the principal governing body in Athens. It was the heartbeat of Athenian democracy. It convened regularly, and any of its tens of thousands of members could attend. Notably, these weren't elected officials or societal elites—they were ordinary Athenian citizens. Major decisions about Athens' future were debated at these meetings, from laws to wars to public projects. Every voice had the right to be heard, and every opinion mattered. *In essence, the fate of Athens lay in the hands of those who chose to attend the Ekklesia.*

Sortition: Another innovative feature of Athenian democracy was sortition, the practice of selecting public officials at random rather than by election. This process ensured that a broad cross-section of society could participate in governance, minimising the risk of entrenched political elites monopolising power. By distributing power among its citizens, Athens hoped to prevent corruption and maintain a balanced representation of its population in decision-making roles.

The Boule: While the Ekklesia was the primary decision-making body, the Boule, or Council of 500, played an essential administrative role. Comprising members chosen by lot, the Boule streamlined decision-making by setting the agenda for the Ekklesia and handled the city's day-to-day operations. It served as a bridge, ensuring that while the populace had the final say, there was an organised system in place to manage daily governance.

Similarly, the Roman Republic, founded in 509 BCE, further advanced the idea of political representation. Senators and consuls were elected by Roman citizens and wielded significant power in the governance of the state. These early Roman politicians navigated the complexities of representation, statecraft, and public debate, laying the groundwork for modern representative democracies. The Roman model also introduced the concept of political factions and parties, as politicians with similar ideals began to align themselves with one another.

The collapse of the Roman Republic and the rise of the Roman Empire under Augustus in 27 BCE signalled a return to centralised, autocratic rule, but the Roman model of political competition and representation would continue to influence future political systems.

Feudalism and the Middle Ages: Lords, Vassals, and the Emergence of Bureaucracy

With the fall of the Roman Empire in the fifth century CE, Europe entered the feudal period, where political power was decentralised and local lords and vassals controlled land and resources. These lords, while technically subjects of a monarch, governed their territories autonomously, with armies and judicial systems of their own. In many ways, they were proto-politicians, negotiating alliances, engaging in warfare, and managing resources.

As monarchs in Europe began to consolidate their power in the High Middle Ages, a more formalised bureaucratic structure emerged to administer kingdoms. Politicians in this era often took the form of court officials, advisers, and ministers who managed state affairs on behalf of kings and queens. The rise of centralised bureaucracies marked the beginning of a distinction between the ruler and the state apparatus, a crucial step in the evolution of modern politics.

The Enlightenment and Revolutions: The Rise of Representative Politics

The political landscape of Europe underwent seismic shifts in the seventeenth and eighteenth centuries, driven by intellectual and ideological movements such as the Enlightenment. Thinkers like John Locke, Jean-Jacques Rousseau, and Montesquieu began to advocate for the principles of popular sovereignty, the separation of powers, and individual rights. The notion that political authority derived from the consent of the governed—rather than divine right—gained traction.

The American Revolution (1775–1783) and the French Revolution (1789–1799) were monumental in reshaping the political landscape and overthrowing monarchies in favour of republican forms of government. Politicians now became the representatives of the people, tasked with enacting the will of the populace. Figures like George Washington, Thomas Jefferson, and Maximilien Robespierre were not just leaders; they were embodiments of new political ideals, fighting for a system where governance was accountable to the people.

The creation of new political systems, particularly the American Constitution, formalised the role of the politician as a representative in a democratic system. In the centuries to follow, this model would spread globally, redefining governance structures everywhere.

The Industrial Revolution and the Growth of Political Parties

The nineteenth century ushered in the Industrial Revolution, transforming economies, societies, and political systems worldwide. With industrialisation came urbanisation and the rise of a working-class population that demanded political representation. This period saw the proliferation of political parties as politicians sought to organise their efforts and rally support for their policies.

The British parliamentary system, with its Whigs and Tories, evolved into the modern party system, and other nations followed suit. Political parties became essential to the functioning of democratic governance, with politicians aligning themselves along ideological lines to contest elections, form governments, and implement policies.

This era also witnessed the expansion of suffrage, with more men—and eventually women—gaining the right to vote. Politicians were no longer representatives of a small elite but of broader segments of the population. Figures like William Gladstone, Benjamin Disraeli, and later Franklin D. Roosevelt and Winston Churchill exemplified the new breed of politician: individuals who could command mass support through oratory, policy, and public appeal.

The Twentieth Century: Politicians as Public Figures

The twentieth century saw the expansion of democratic governance across the globe, though it was also marked by the rise of totalitarian regimes that attempted to suppress political pluralism. In democratic nations, however, politicians became not only representatives of the people but also public figures in a mass-media age. The advent of radio, television, and eventually the Internet transformed how politicians interacted with the public. They became more than just lawmakers; they became celebrities, wielding influence not only through policy but through their personal charisma and media presence.

In the aftermath of World War II, institutions such as the United Nations and the European Union (EU) further changed the political landscape. Politicians were now not only national figures but also global actors, negotiating on the world stage. Figures such as John F. Kennedy, Margaret Thatcher, and Nelson Mandela transcended national boundaries, influencing global political discourse.

Contemporary Politics: The Centrality of the Politician in the Information Age

Today, politicians are central to governance in ways that would have been unimaginable in earlier eras. With 24-hour news cycles and the rise of social media, political figures are constantly in the public eye. Their every move is scrutinised, and public perception plays a significant role in their ability to govern. This has led to the rise of a new type of politician—one who must not only navigate complex political systems but also engage with the public regularly.

In the modern era, politicians are more than just representatives or lawmakers; they are managers of public relations, influencers of opinion, and key players in a globalised world where domestic issues often have international repercussions. Figures like Barack

Obama, Narendra Modi, and Angela Merkel demonstrate how politicians have become central figures not only in governance but in shaping the cultural and societal narratives of their time.

The Role of Bureaucracy

Behind the elected officials operates the bureaucracy—an often vast apparatus responsible for the day-to-day administration of the state. Bureaucracies are meant to implement the policies decided by elected officials and are essential for maintaining continuity and providing services regardless of changes in leadership. However, bureaucracies can also become unwieldy and inefficient, and their permanence and power can lead to a lack of accountability and responsiveness to public needs.

In India, the bureaucracy is termed as the committed bureaucracy, in other words, 'His Master's Voice'. When these two most important institutions lose their moral compass and the fence starts eating the grass, the need for reformation stands beyond doubt.

From Chiefs to Politicians: A Journey of Power and Representation

The evolution of political structures and the role of politicians is a story of the increasing complexity of governance. From tribal elders to kings, senators, and modern-day presidents and prime ministers, politicians have become a vital part of how societies organise themselves. Politicians are the face of governance, representing the hopes, aspirations, and fears of the people they serve.

As political disillusionment grows, citizens worldwide feel alienated from political processes, and trust in institutions wanes. Drawing from the wisdom of the past provides a valuable lens through which to view our current political landscape. The principles of active citizen participation and accountability are timeless. By integrating these ideals into our modern context, we can address contemporary challenges more effectively.

The digital age presents both opportunities and challenges for democracy. Technology can facilitate greater citizen participation through online voting platforms, virtual town halls, and social media engagement. However, it also brings risks like misinformation, echo chambers, and data privacy concerns.

Today's most pressing challenges—climate change, pandemics, and economic inequality—transcend national borders. Traditional political structures often struggle to address these complex, global issues effectively.

The Athenian emphasis on collective decision-making and civic duty offers a blueprint for modern collaboration. Just as Athenians gathered to discuss matters affecting their city-state, global citizens can come together to find common solutions. This requires new forms of international cooperation and a willingness to look beyond individual or national interests.

Reconnecting citizens with the political process revitalises democracy. It fosters a governance system that is not only more responsive and equitable but also more capable of tackling the complex issues that define our time.

CHAPTER 2

◆◆◆

The Role of Politicians in Modern Politics

In modern politics, the role of politicians is central yet often contested. As the world becomes more complex, interconnected, and technologically driven, the role of those we elect to represent and lead us is under greater scrutiny. Politicians have traditionally held power as representatives, decision-makers, and intermediaries, but the demands of the twenty-first century present new challenges. With the rise of populism, deepening societal divides, and a growing distrust in political institutions, politicians must navigate an increasingly complicated landscape. This chapter expands on these themes, delving into the evolving nature of political leadership and exploring the profound impact that changing global dynamics have on governance.

Politicians as Representatives: A Balancing Act

From Classical Representation to Modern Complexities, the concept of political representation is deeply embedded in democratic theory. As far back as the Ancient Greeks, democratic systems sought ways for citizens to have a say in decision-making processes. While Athenian democracy allowed for direct participation, modern representative democracies involve elected politicians who act on behalf of their constituents. The role of a representative is complex, requiring politicians to navigate the often-conflicting interests of their voter base.

In modern times, this traditional role has become more nuanced. As societies have become more diverse, politicians are increasingly expected to represent a broader spectrum of views and interests. In countries like India and the United States, for instance, elected officials represent constituencies that vary widely in terms of ethnicity, religion, socioeconomic status, and political ideology. These representatives must balance conflicting interests, often in the context of deeply divided societies.

The Crisis of Representation: Who Do Politicians Really Serve?

A central criticism of modern politics is that elected officials often fail to represent the true interests of their constituents. The growing influence of corporate donations, lobbying groups, and political action committees (PACs) has led many to argue that politicians serve the interests of the wealthy elite rather than the general public. This is particularly evident in countries with expensive electoral systems, such as the United States, where campaigns are heavily funded by corporate donations. The

influence of 'big money' in politics raises concerns about the true efficacy of representation.

The global surge in populist movements is, in part, a reaction to this crisis of representation. Populist leaders position themselves as outsiders who stand up to the political elite, claiming to represent the 'true' will of the people. Donald Trump's rise in the US, Nigel Farage's role in Brexit, and Narendra Modi's electoral success in India illustrate how populist figures capitalise on public disillusionment with traditional political elites. However, populist leaders often concentrate power in their hands, bypassing established institutions and undermining the checks and balances essential to democratic governance.

The Politics of Identity: Representation in Diverse Societies

Modern societies are increasingly multicultural and multiracial, requiring politicians to navigate the complexities of identity politics. Issues of race, gender, and religion now dominate political discourse in many countries, and politicians are expected to engage with these matters thoughtfully and sensitively. In the United States, for example, the growing influence of minority groups has prompted shifts in the platforms of both major political parties. Democratic politicians, in particular, have increasingly embraced progressive policies on issues such as LGBTQ+ (lesbian, gay, bisexual, transgender, queer/questioning, and more) rights, immigration reform, and racial justice.

However, identity politics has also polarised the political landscape. On the right, some politicians have tapped into fears of demographic change, rallying support around nationalist and anti-immigrant sentiments. This has led to growing divisions within societies, as exemplified by the rise of far-right political parties in Europe, such as the Alternative for Germany (AfD) and France's National Rally.

In this increasingly polarised environment, the role of politicians as representatives has become more challenging than ever. They must navigate deep societal divides, represent diverse communities, and build consensus, all while maintaining their political legitimacy.

Politicians as Decision-Makers: Navigating the Modern Political Maze

Complexity in Decision-Making: Governance in the Twenty-First Century

The task of governing a modern state is more complex than at any point in history. As political, social, and economic systems become more interconnected, the decisions politicians make are subject to a myriad of influences, both domestic and international. Issues such as climate change, globalisation, and digitalisation have added layers of complexity to the decision-making process. Politicians are no longer just dealing with local or national concerns; they must also consider global ramifications.

For instance, when policymakers make decisions about the environment, they must balance short-term economic growth with long-term sustainability. This is particularly true in developing nations, where leaders often face difficult choices between exploiting natural resources for economic gain and preserving those resources for future generations. In Brazil, political leaders have struggled to balance the demands of the agricultural and logging industries with the need to protect the Amazon rainforest, a critical global carbon sink.

At the same time, the rise of international organisations, trade agreements, and multinational corporations has further complicated political decision-making. Politicians are increasingly constrained by international treaties and the global economy. For example, decisions about tax policy in one country can have far-reaching effects on global financial markets, leading politicians to coordinate with other countries in ways that would have been unimaginable just a few decades ago.

Navigating Public Expectations: Populism and Technocracy

In addition to these global complexities, politicians must contend with the growing demand for instant results from their electorates. The rise of social media has given the public unprecedented access to politicians and has amplified expectations for immediate action on pressing issues. Citizens increasingly demand transparency, accountability, and rapid responses to crises,creating pressure on politicians to deliver quick solutions to deep-seated problems.

This dynamic has fuelled the rise of populism, which thrives on offering simple, clear-cut solutions to complex problems. Populist leaders often promise to bypass bureaucratic red tape, ignore expert advice, and deliver decisive action. However, the effectiveness of these 'quick fixes' is debatable, as long-term challenges such as economic inequality, climate change, and healthcare reform often require nuanced, well-thought-out policies.

In contrast, technocratic leaders emphasise the need for expert-led governance. Figures like Angela Merkel in Germany and Mario Draghi in Italy have championed evidence-based decision-making, relying heavily on scientific data and economic models to guide policy. Technocracy offers a counter-narrative to populism, suggesting that complex problems require expert solutions rather than populist rhetoric. However, technocratic governance can sometimes alienate the general public, as decisions made by experts are perceived as detached from the everyday concerns of ordinary citizens.

Case Study: The COVID-19 Pandemic and Political Decision-Making

The COVID-19 (coronavirus disease of 2019) pandemic provides a powerful example of the complex role politicians play as decision-makers. Faced with a global health crisis, political leaders had to make swift decisions on issues ranging from public health to economic relief, often with limited information and uncertain outcomes. The pandemic highlighted the need for politicians to balance expert advice with the realities of governance as they weighed the economic costs of lockdowns against the need to protect public health.

In countries like New Zealand, Prime Minister Jacinda Ardern was praised for her swift and decisive response to the pandemic, implementing strict lockdown measures early on. Her government prioritised public health over short-term economic concerns, a decision that helped the country contain the virus more effectively than many other nations. In contrast, leaders like Brazil's Jair Bolsonaro downplayed the severity of the virus, prioritising economic interests and rejecting expert advice, leading to widespread criticism of their handling of the crisis.

The pandemic also underscored the interconnectedness of global decision-making. Politicians had to work together across borders, coordinating vaccine distribution, managing supply chains, and sharing public health data. This global cooperation demonstrated the importance of diplomacy and international collaboration in modern political decision-making.

Politicians as Intermediaries: Bridging the Gap Between Government and People

Communicating Policy in the Information Age

In the digital age, politicians act not only as decision-makers but also as intermediaries who communicate policies and political positions to the public. The rise of 24-hour news cycles, social media, and citizen journalism has transformed the relationship between politicians and the electorate. In many ways, modern politicians must be as adept at managing their public image as they are at crafting policy.

Politicians today have unprecedented access to the public via social media platforms like Twitter, Instagram, and TikTok, where they can bypass traditional media outlets to deliver their message directly to voters. This has democratised political communication but has also created new challenges. The immediacy of digital communication means that politicians must respond quickly to breaking news and scandals, often without the luxury of carefully crafted statements. The rapid spread of misinformation further complicates this dynamic, as politicians are now tasked with debunking false claims promptly.

One of the most prominent examples of this shift is former US President Donald Trump, who famously used Twitter as his primary mode of communication. By speaking directly to his followers, Trump was able to galvanise support for his agenda and sidestep the critical coverage he often received from mainstream media outlets. While his use of social media was revolutionary, it also contributed to political polarisation and the spread of misinformation, leading to increased scrutiny of how politicians communicate in the digital age.

The Role of Political Spin and Public Relations

The rise of professional political communication teams has also changed the role of politicians as intermediaries. Today, most politicians rely on teams of advisers, speech writers, and public relations specialists to manage their public image and messaging. This professionalisation of political communication has allowed politicians to craft more effective and targeted messages, but it has also led to accusations that modern politics is more about optics than substance.

Political 'spin'—the strategic presentation of information to shape public perception has become an integral part of modern political communication. Spin doctors work behind the scenes to frame political decisions in the most favourable light, often obscuring the complexities of policy in favour of simplistic soundbites. While this can help politicians connect with voters on an emotional level, it also raises concerns about transparency and the manipulation of public opinion.

A notable example of political spin is the use of 'talking points' during elections or crises. These carefully crafted statements are designed to be repeated by politicians and their supporters across media platforms, creating a consistent narrative that can dominate the news cycle. While talking points can help politicians stay on message, they also contribute to the perception that modern political discourse is shallow and formulaic.

Case Study: Social Media, Political Communication, and Polarisation

Social media's impact on politics is a topic of growing concern. While platforms like Facebook and Twitter allow for direct communication between politicians and the public, they also contribute to political polarisation by creating echo chambers where individuals are exposed only to views that reinforce their pre-existing beliefs.

The role of social media in politics was starkly highlighted during the 2016 US presidential election, where misinformation and targeted advertising campaigns, particularly by foreign actors, played a significant role in shaping public opinion. The Cambridge Analytica scandal revealed how data analytics and social media algorithms could be used to micro-target voters with tailored messages, raising ethical questions about the role of technology in modern elections.

Moreover, social media has amplified political divisions, as platforms reward extreme views that generate engagement.

Politicians who adopt more polarising rhetoric often gain more visibility on these platforms, contributing to the fragmentation of public discourse. This trend has been observed globally, from the rise of far-right leaders in Europe to the deepening political divides in countries like Brazil, India, and the United States.

The Erosion of Trust in Politicians and Political Institutions

Declining Trust in Political Systems: A Global Trend

One of the most pressing issues in modern politics is the erosion of trust in politicians and political institutions. Across the world, public confidence in political leaders, legislatures, and governments is at an all-time low. A 2019 Pew Research Centre survey found that just 17% of Americans trusted their government to do the right thing most of the time—a sharp decline from the 73% who expressed similar sentiments in 1958. Similar trends can be observed across Europe, Latin America, and parts of Asia.

A little-realised fact of history is that the world has been at peace for only 268 years out of 3400 years, or just eight per cent of its recorded history. Since its birth in 1776, the US has been at war for 230 years out of 248, or 93 per cent, fighting on others' territories. Civilian casualties have been entirely on the others' side except for the 9/11 terrorist attack. The US has over 800 military bases around the world, more than the embassies it has, all in the garb of maintaining world stability and peace, aka protecting its hegemonic position. Diplomacy is a tool for peace and negotiations; military bases are tools of violence that breed more violence. Since 1816, there hasn't been a single point in time when the world has not been in a state of war somewhere. People do not decide to go to war; the elected political leadership does. Politicians rarely suffer; people do—always.

The West, with its self-acclaimed high moral standing of human rights, democracy, and law-based global order, has been the cause of the worst human suffering—the First World War, the Second World War, the Vietnam War, the Bosnia War, the Iraq War, the Afghanistan Wars, the ongoing Russia-Ukraine War, and the Israel-Hamas War.

The US, the global policeman and the self-proclaimed keeper of human values of democracy and freedom, has been the singular cause of most wars around the globe.

While the list is unending, we will look at some examples.

Regime Change: The US has been constantly involved in regime changes when it suited its interests. It has no moral standards that guide its decisions, and it justifies such actions on some frivolous grounds. Democratic governments were overthrown while they continued to support suppressive and despotic regimes. The US interference in South America is too numerous to repeat here. In all such cases, it resulted in serious consequences for the people of the region.

In Iran in 1953, the US orchestrated a coup to overthrow democratically elected Prime Minister Mohammad Mosaddegh, reinstating the Shah, who ruled with an authoritarian regime. Eventually, the Shah was overthrown in a coup led by clerics. The world is facing the consequences of this act, as we can see in the Middle East and the Arab world, which is on the brink of disaster.

Middle East Policy and Oil Interests: Throughout the twentieth century, US foreign policy in the Middle East has prioritised access to oil and strategic dominance over democratic values, leading to long-term geopolitical instability and resentment towards the US

Vietnam War (1955–1975): The Vietnam War was a manifestation of Picolo's law of stupidity. The US, which, during the Second World War, had supported the rights of colonies to decide their own governance, much to the chagrin of Winston Churchill, ended up financing the colonial French in Vietnam. It is estimated that the US dropped between seven and thirteen million tonnes of bombs on Indo-China, three times more than what was dropped in the entire Second World War. It killed an estimated two million people. The 'Domino Theory' on the expansion of communism in Southeast Asia, the *casus belli* of war, proved to be wrong. It was the public protest that brought that war to an end when the brutality that was being inflicted on innocent Vietnamese was exposed.

When we talk of mistrust and politicians, McNamara shines bright in the context of Vietnam. To make up for the escalating demands of manpower in Vietnam, McNamara came up with a despicable plan. He lowered the recruitment standards to recruit low-IQ candidates who were mentally and physically unfit to be soldiers. They came to be known as 'McNamara's Morons'. They even included some men with autistic disabilities, etc., who could not even read or write, but mysteriously passed the written tests!

McNamara believed he could win the war in Vietnam through the use of advanced technology and computerised analysis. Hamilton Gregory, author of *McNamara's Folly: The Use of Low-IQ Troops in the Vietnam War*, writes that he thought one could turn below-average soldiers into above-average soldiers through the use of technology and learning by use of videotapes. The casualty rates of these troops were three times higher than the regular troops.

That the politicians did this is unsurprising; that the military leadership, fully understanding the implications, accepted it was a tragedy.

Why this is so alarming is that, as author Hamilton Gregory points out, enough loopholes were left to enable the politically influential middle class to avoid the draft for political expediency. As he says, one senator's son was medically exempted from the draft for wearing braces on his teeth! This project, suitably sugar-coated, targeted the poor class who could not complain or protest. Their lot after the war was no better than promised. Trust or mistrust?

The Iraq War 2003: The US launched an unprovoked, UN (United Nations)-opposed war against international law on fabricated and false justification of weapons of mass destruction in Iraq. The war sent the region into turmoil, resulting in the rise of the Islamic State. More than 30 countries joined them as a coalition of the willing in this illegal war. It killed an estimated million Iraqis.

Madeleine Albright was the US Secretary of State from 1997 to 2001. During an interview, she was asked, 'Half a million children have died in Iraq, more than children who died in Hiroshima. Is the price worth it?'

Madeleine replied, 'I think it is a very hard choice, but the price, we see the price is worth it.'

She is a tragic reflection of the mentality of the West. What sanity could be expected from her and others if half a million children's lives can be dismissed without batting an eyelid? Would it be the same if half of them were American or European children?

The Syrian mess is a result of a power play between the US and Russia at the whims of the elected few that have created a humanitarian crisis and killed hundreds of thousands. Along with the US, Russia, China, North Korea, and Iran have destabilised the world as the UN watches helplessly, reducing it to a debating platform. There is no dearth of suppressive regimes in the world.

Today, protests are taking place all over America and Europe against the Israel-Hamas War, yet the war goes on escalating for political expediency. In all this, the military-industrial complex of the West is having the last laugh, as are many politicians.

Interestingly, hundreds of children and people die year after year in gun-related violence in the US. Yet, the politicians fail to institute stricter gun control laws because of the pressure of the gun lobby, which finances campaigns on both sides. So much for the concern of public safety.

Barring World War II, the rest of the wars could be called wars of choice, not necessity. The US attacked Afghanistan post 9/11. None of the 9/11 terrorists was an Afghan or an Iraqi. Two decades later, after an estimated over a hundred thousand Afghans were killed, the Taliban is back in power with American military equipment, and the state of Afghanistan is worse than before the war.

Before the world could reconcile to the Afghanistan fiasco, President Biden had engineered another war, the Russia-Ukraine War. It is now seriously embroiled in two major wars that have impacted the entire humanity: the Russia-Ukraine War and the Israeli-Hamas War. These two wars have ignited the spectre of global war and brought the world closer to a nuclear war than ever before.

Similarly, the United Kingdom (UK), another major actor, has been a violator of international values, starting from misleading its people and joining the illegal war on Iraq in 2003.

China, Iran, and North Korea brutally suppress their people, the first on communist ideology and the second on theological ideology. North Korea remains a family enterprise in this modern world, threatening the world with nuclear weapons.

The world is facing a catastrophe due to climate change. The West, the major exploiter of natural resources and the emitter of chlorofluorocarbon (CFC) gases, has repeatedly failed to meet its obligations in every way. Climate conferences are all talk and little action. Their duplicity is more than evident. Some politicians even challenge the existence of global warming, as some even challenge that the holocaust ever happened! It is young people like Greta Thunberg who are leading the charge against the inaction of the elected leadership.

The UN, which came into existence after the Second World War, has become redundant and has failed to prevent wars because the powerful five have the unjustified veto power to veto anything that is against their national interests despite its gravity against international law. This needs to go.

India, the largest democracy, makes for an interesting case study. It is in India that a barely literate woman with no experience in politics or governance can be pitch-forked from the kitchen to the cabinet as a chief minister of a state. It is also the only country where an illiterate dacoit queen can become a member of parliament.

Crime and politics are congenital twins across countries. In the 2019 general elections in India, over 40 per cent of elected members of parliament (MPs) had criminal cases against them, varying from intimidation and trespassing to murder. In some cases, they numbered over a hundred. As per the survey conducted for the 2019 Lok Sabha elections, the chances of winning for a candidate with a criminal record were 15.5 per cent, whereas for a candidate with a clean background, they were 4.7 per cent. India is a country where a person from inside the prison can contest elections, while one from inside the prison cannot vote in an election. It is a tragedy that two undertrial separatists contested elections for MP from inside the prison and won in 2024.

Indian politics takes the cake. The politicians here see jail terms as medals of honour. It will take less than one hand to count on the fingertips the number of politicians who have ever been punished for the gravest of crimes despite special courts. The Indian public, while seen to be politically aware and astute, lines up the roads in lakhs to welcome a criminal politician released from jail.

It is a tragicomedy that a person needs a qualification to be appointed a peon, whereas no educational qualification is required to be a minister at any level. All this cannot be the virtues of democracy and strike at the trust between politicians and the right-thinking public.

The tables below show the relative trust of professions and the enduring nature of the trust deficit in politicians across the globe.

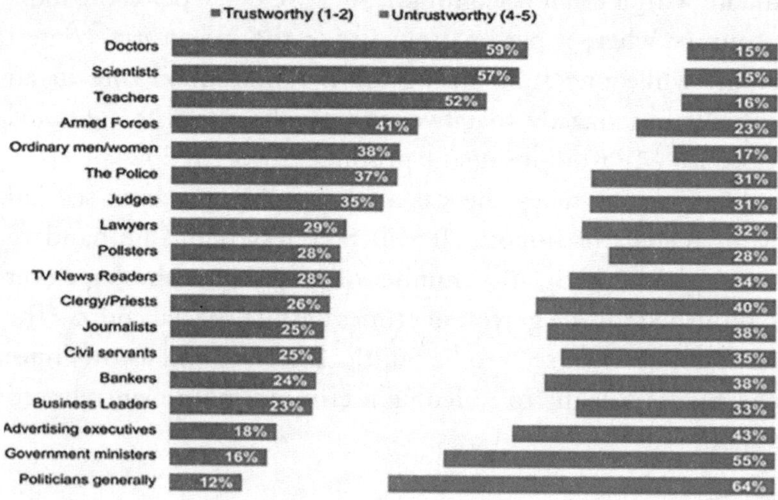

Global Trust in Professions Index

	Trustworthy (1-2)	2021	2019	2018
Doctors	58%	64%	57%	55%
Scientists	57%	61%	59%	59%
Teachers	51%	55%	53%	52%
Armed Forces	42%	44%	44%	43%
Ordinary men/women	37%	38%	38%	37%
The Police	37%	40%	38%	39%
Judges	35%	37%	33%	32%
Lawyers	29%	30%	28%	25%
Television news readers	28%	27%	25%	24%
Pollsters	27%	25%	23%	23%
Clergy/Priests	26%	26%	24%	21%
Civil Servants	26%	25%	23%	24%
Journalists	25%	23%	22%	21%
Bankers	24%	23%	21%	20%
Business Leaders	23%	23%	22%	22%
Advertising executives	17%	15%	13%	13%
Government ministers	16%	15%	13%	12%
Politicians generally	12%	10%	10%	9%

Trends Over Time

This decline in trust can be attributed to a variety of factors. Scandals involving corruption, nepotism, and financial mismanagement have eroded public confidence in politicians. In many countries, politicians are perceived as being out of touch with the everyday concerns of ordinary citizens, more interested in enriching themselves and maintaining power than in serving the public.

In addition to scandals, the perceived inefficiency of political systems has contributed to declining trust. Gridlock in legislatures, the failure to address pressing issues like climate change and income inequality, and the rise of partisan politics have led many to question the effectiveness of their leaders. This disillusionment has been further fuelled by economic instability, the hollowing out of the middle class, and the growing gap between rich and poor.

The Impact of Scandals and Corruption

Political scandals have been a major driver of declining trust in politicians. From the Watergate scandal in the United States to the Petrobras corruption scandal in Brazil, instances of political corruption have damaged the reputations of political leaders and undermined the legitimacy of political institutions.

The impact of political corruption is particularly acute in developing countries, where weak institutions and limited oversight create opportunities for graft and abuse of power. In countries like South Africa, politicians have been accused of using public funds for personal enrichment, contributing to widespread cynicism about the political process. Corruption scandals also have a broader impact on governance, as they can delay the implementation of policies and exacerbate social inequalities.

Even in established democracies, scandals involving politicians' personal lives or financial dealings can have serious consequences. For example, the resignation of British Prime Minister Boris Johnson in 2022, following a series of ethical and legal controversies, illustrates how political scandals can erode public confidence in leadership.

Case Study: The Rise of Populism as a Response to Political Disillusionment

The rise of populism is closely linked to declining trust in politicians and political institutions. Populist leaders often position themselves as the antidote to political corruption, promising to 'drain the swamp' and restore power to the people. This message resonates with voters who feel alienated from traditional political elites and disillusioned with the existing system.

One of the defining characteristics of populist leaders is their appeal to a sense of grievance. They claim to represent the 'forgotten' people, whether working-class voters in post-industrial towns or rural communities left behind by globalisation. Populists often frame politics as a battle between the virtuous people and the corrupt elite, using this narrative to justify their often authoritarian tactics.

Leaders like Hungary's Viktor Orbán, Brazil's Jair Bolsonaro, and the Philippines' Rodrigo Duterte have all risen to power by positioning themselves as outsiders who will shake up the political establishment. While these leaders enjoy widespread support from segments of the population, their critics argue that they undermine democratic norms and erode the checks and balances that prevent the abuse of power.

The Future of Political Leadership: Adapting to Change

Technology and the Transformation of Political Campaigning

Technology has fundamentally changed the way politicians

campaign, communicate, and govern. The advent of big data, artificial intelligence (AI), and digital marketing has revolutionised election campaigns, allowing candidates to micro-target voters with personalised messages. Political campaigns now rely on vast amounts of data to identify key voting blocs, analyse public opinion, and craft targeted advertising.

The use of algorithms and predictive analytics has made political campaigns more efficient, but it has also raised concerns about privacy and the manipulation of public opinion. The Cambridge Analytica scandal, in which data from millions of Facebook users was harvested without their consent for political purposes, exposed the potential dangers of using data analytics in politics.

Moreover, the rise of deepfakes, disinformation campaigns, and cyberattacks poses new challenges for political leaders. Politicians must now navigate an increasingly complex digital landscape where malicious actors can spread false information or interfere in elections. Ensuring the integrity of the democratic process in the face of these challenges will be one of the key tasks for political leaders in the twenty-first century.

The Impact of Climate Change on Political Leadership

Climate change is arguably the most pressing issue facing political leaders today. The scientific consensus is clear: the planet is warming, and human activity is the primary driver. As the effects of climate change become more pronounced, politicians are under increasing pressure to take decisive action to mitigate its impacts.

However, climate change presents unique challenges for political leaders. It requires long-term thinking and global cooperation, both of which are difficult to achieve in a political system that often prioritises short-term gains. In many countries, politicians are reluctant to enact the radical changes needed to address climate change, fearing backlash from voters or powerful interest groups.

The fossil fuel industry, in particular, wields significant influence in many countries, making it difficult for politicians to push through ambitious climate policies.

Despite these challenges, some political leaders have made significant strides in addressing climate change. In Europe, the European Green Deal aims to make the continent carbon-neutral by 2050, while countries like Costa Rica have implemented ambitious environmental policies that prioritise sustainability. The success of these efforts will depend on the willingness of politicians to embrace bold solutions and the ability of international institutions to foster global cooperation.

The Rise of Non-Traditional Political Actors

In recent years, non-traditional political actors, such as activists, celebrities, and business leaders, have played an increasingly prominent role in shaping political discourse. Figures like Elon Musk, Greta Thunberg, and Malala Yousafzai have garnered significant media attention and public support, often rivalling or surpassing traditional politicians in terms of influence.

These non-traditional actors use their platforms to advocate for specific causes, bypassing the traditional political process. For example, Greta Thunberg's school strikes for climate change galvanised a global youth movement, putting pressure on governments to take more aggressive action on environmental issues. Similarly, tech entrepreneurs like Elon Musk have used their influence to push for advancements in renewable energy and space exploration.

While these figures have been praised for their advocacy, their rise also raises questions about the future of political leadership. If traditional politicians are increasingly sidelined by non-traditional actors, what does this mean for the future of representative democracy? Will political power shift away from elected officials and toward those with access to media platforms and financial resources?

Political Parties: Pillars of Democracy or Agents of Discord?

In the intricate tapestry of democracy, political parties emerge as key players, influencing the responsiveness of governments to the ever-shifting preferences of the people. However, in real life, political parties, in the obscene pursuit of power, cross all boundaries of ethical conduct.

Robert Dahl asserts that the 'continuing responsiveness of the government to the preferences of its citizens' stands as a defining characteristic of democracy. The underlying assumption is that political parties act as conduits, channelling the collective will of the people into tangible policy outcomes. Yet, the landscape is far from monolithic, with dissenting voices challenging the presumed harmony between parties and democratic ideals.

Contrarily, a contrasting viewpoint paints parties as potential disruptors of democratic harmony. According to this perspective, parties, in their relentless pursuit of electoral triumphs, are prepared to jettison all ethics and norms and overlook the genuine implementation of policies that truly mirror the desires of the populace. In this light, parties become instruments of power consolidation rather than vehicles of substantive change in tune with the preferences of the electorate.

The internal dynamics of political parties and the dynamics of coalition government further complicate this narrative. Parties can exhibit a unified front or internal divisions, adding another layer to their impact on democratic processes. The interplay between these dimensions spawns a rich array of theories, each seeking to position political parties in the complex spectrum of democratic governance.

In navigating this intellectual terrain, scholars and theorists grapple with critical questions. Do political parties serve as guardians of democratic ideals, translating popular will into tangible policy outcomes? Or do they, in their quest for power, inadvertently sow seeds of discord, leading to a disconnect between government actions and citizen preferences? Worse, as the American and the Indian general elections of 2024 showed, political parties are prepared to sow communal disharmony through actual or fake narratives in pursuit of power or simply to discredit the government in power. The opposition takes its job too seriously, opposing for the opposition's sake, opposing even those policies which they were pursuing when they were in power, simply because it is fructifying now, and the government of the day would get the credit.

As the discourse on political parties and democracy unfolds, the intricate dance between theory and practice continues. The true essence of political parties in a democracy remains an enigma, a puzzle that scholars, policymakers, and citizens alike seek to decipher for the continued evolution of democratic governance.

The Evolving Role of Politicians in the Twenty-First Century

The role of politicians in modern politics is multifaceted and constantly evolving. As representatives, decision-makers, and intermediaries, politicians are tasked with balancing the interests of diverse constituencies, navigating complex global issues, and communicating their policies to an increasingly sceptical public. However, the rise of new political actors, technological advancements, and growing distrust in political institutions have challenged the traditional role of politicians.

In the face of these challenges, politicians must adapt to remain relevant and effective. Whether through embracing new technologies, addressing public disillusionment, or finding innovative ways to connect with their constituents, the future of political leadership will depend on politicians' ability to navigate the rapidly changing landscape of modern governance.

As we move further into the twenty-first century, the question remains: can traditional politicians keep pace with the demands of a rapidly changing world, or will non-traditional actors take their place in shaping the future of politics? The answer will have profound implications for the future of democracy and governance around the globe.

CHAPTER 3

◆◆◆

Political Systems and Power Dynamics

The separation of powers is a hallmark of modern democracies, designed to prevent the concentration of power and provide a system of checks and balances among the legislative, executive, and judicial branches of government. This model was inspired by Montesquieu's political theory and has been integral in maintaining a balance of power that prevents any one branch from dominating the government.

The chapter will explore different forms of government, power structures, and how the concentration of power in the hands of politicians affects the governance process.

Political systems are the frameworks through which societies organise power, authority, and decision-making. At their core, these systems revolve around how power is distributed—whether through centralised leadership or shared governance—and the extent to which politicians, as representatives or decision-makers, wield influence. While politicians play a critical role in shaping policies and directing governments, their concentration of power can also expose inherent flaws and limitations in governance.

This chapter will examine how different political systems manage the distribution of power, exploring both democratic and authoritarian models. It will analyse the implications of politician-centric governance, shedding light on the limitations that arise when authority is concentrated in the hands of a few individuals. By understanding the power dynamics within political systems, we gain a clearer picture of the strengths and weaknesses that define contemporary governance.

Power Distribution in Political Systems: A Spectrum

Democratic Systems: Shared Power and Accountability

At one end of the spectrum lies democracy, where power is dispersed across institutions and individuals to prevent the concentration of authority. In democratic political systems, the principle of popular sovereignty ensures that power ultimately rests with the people. Citizens elect representatives, who, in turn, make decisions on their behalf. This dispersal of power aims to create a system of checks and balances to limit any single individual's or institution's control.

In parliamentary systems, such as those found in the United Kingdom or India, the executive branch is derived from the legislature, with the prime minister serving as the head of government. Power is shared between elected representatives, and politicians are accountable to their constituents through regular elections. The separation of powers between the executive, legislative, and judicial branches is a hallmark of democratic governance.

In presidential systems, such as that of the United States, power is separated between an independently elected executive (the president) and a legislature. This division creates a balance, where politicians in different branches of government must cooperate while acting as a check on each other's power. Citizens participate directly in choosing their leaders, and elected officials must operate within a legal framework defined by a constitution.

However, even in democratic systems, power can become concentrated in the hands of certain politicians or political parties, especially when institutional safeguards weaken. As a result, democracy, while theoretically a system that prevents over-centralisation, can still face challenges when power dynamics shift toward entrenched political elites.

Authoritarian Systems: Centralised Power and Limited Accountability

At the other end of the spectrum, authoritarian political systems concentrate power in the hands of a single leader or ruling party. In these systems, decision-making authority is heavily centralised, with limited input from citizens or representative institutions. Power flows from the top down, and political leaders often use coercive means to maintain control and suppress opposition.

Authoritarian regimes, such as those found in North Korea, Saudi Arabia, or historically in various military dictatorships like Pakistan for the better part of their existence, restrict political pluralism and limit the role of political opposition. In these systems, politicians often function more as instruments of the ruling leader than as independent decision-makers. Political power is not distributed but hoarded, and rulers are not held accountable to the public.

The concentration of power in authoritarian systems results in a lack of transparency, and politicians are not required to justify their actions to the public. This power dynamic also leads to inefficiencies in governance, as decision-making is confined to a narrow circle of elites. Without open debate, dissent, or accountability mechanisms, authoritarian regimes are prone to corruption and policy failures that can go unchecked for long periods.

Forms of Power: Hard, Soft, and Structural

Political power is not monolithic. Different forms of power—

hard, soft, and structural—are used by politicians and institutions to influence decision-making, maintain control, and shape the political environment.

Hard Power: Coercive Control

Hard power refers to the use of force, coercion, or material incentives to compel compliance. In political systems, hard power is often exercised through laws, military action, police forces, and economic sanctions. Authoritarian regimes are more likely to rely on hard power, using repressive state apparatuses to maintain control and silence dissent.

However, even democratic systems employ hard power. Governments use law enforcement to maintain order and military force to protect national security. While hard power is necessary for the functioning of any state, its misuse by politicians can lead to authoritarian tendencies even within democratic systems, undermining civil liberties and individual rights.

Soft Power: Persuasion and Influence

In contrast, soft power is the ability to shape the preferences and actions of others through attraction, persuasion, and the promotion of values or ideologies. Politicians often rely on soft power to build public support for their policies or win elections. This can be seen in political campaigns, where leaders appeal to voters through speeches, debates, and media appearances.

Internationally, soft power is used by nations to influence global politics. Countries like the United States and China invest heavily in cultural diplomacy, education, and media to shape global public opinion in their favour.

In democratic systems, politicians' ability to wield soft power is crucial for navigating the complex dynamics of governance. They must persuade other branches of government, political parties, and, most importantly, the electorate to support their policies. However, the rise of media manipulation and disinformation poses significant challenges to the effective use of soft power in the political arena.

Structural Power: The Power of Institutions

Structural power refers to the rules, laws, and institutions that shape the political environment and determine how power is distributed. Politicians operating within any system must navigate this structural power as it defines the limits and opportunities for political action.

In democracies, constitutions, legal frameworks, and political institutions establish the rules of governance. These structures help prevent the over-concentration of power by setting up mechanisms of checks and balances, such as the judiciary's ability to review executive actions or the legislative branch's power to pass laws.

In contrast, in authoritarian regimes, structural power is often manipulated to entrench the ruling elite. Constitutions may be rewritten or ignored to consolidate power, and legal institutions may be used to persecute political opponents or suppress dissent. Structural power in these systems reinforces the dominance of the few over the many.

The Inherent Limitations of Politician-Centric Governance

Politicians as Gatekeepers of Power

In most political systems, politicians are the gatekeepers of power, whether they are elected representatives in democracies or ruling elites in authoritarian regimes. The concentration of power in the hands of politicians means that they play a critical role in shaping laws, policies, and national priorities. However, this central role also comes with inherent limitations.

In politician-centric systems, decision-making is often reactive rather than proactive. Politicians may prioritise short-term political gains, focusing on issues that will help them win the next election or maintain their power, rather than addressing long-term challenges such as climate change, social inequality, or economic reform. The short electoral cycle in democracies reinforces this dynamic, as politicians are incentivised to focus on immediate issues that resonate with voters.

Corruption and Self-Interest

One of the most significant limitations of politician-centric governance is the potential for corruption and self-interest. When power is concentrated in the hands of a few, there is a higher risk that politicians will use their authority for personal gain or the benefit of a small elite rather than serving the broader interests of the public.

Corruption can manifest in many forms, from bribery and embezzlement to cronyism and nepotism. In both democratic and authoritarian systems, politicians who wield significant power without sufficient oversight are prone to abusing their position for personal or political benefit.

The Disconnect Between Politicians and the Public

Another limitation of politician-centric governance is the potential disconnect between politicians and the people they are meant to represent. In many cases, politicians come from elite backgrounds, have limited experience with the challenges faced by ordinary citizens, or are insulated from public opinion by bureaucratic structures.

In democratic systems, this disconnect can lead to public disillusionment and disengagement. When citizens feel that their voices are not being heard or that politicians are unresponsive to their needs, voter turnout declines, and trust in political institutions erodes. This creates a vicious cycle where politicians become less accountable, and citizens become less engaged in the political process.

In authoritarian systems, the disconnect between rulers and the ruled is often more pronounced, as leaders are not subject to the same checks and balances as in democracies. Without electoral accountability, authoritarian politicians may prioritise their interests or those of their inner circle rather than addressing the needs of the broader population.

Moving Beyond Politician-Centric Governance: New Models of Power Distribution

Technocratic Governance: Expert-Led Decision Making

In response to the limitations of politician-centric governance, some have advocated for technocratic governance, where decision-making is entrusted to experts in specific fields rather than elected politicians. Technocrats, such as economists, scientists, and engineers, are seen as better equipped to handle complex issues like climate change, public health, and economic policy.

In this model, politicians still play a role in setting broad policy goals, but day-to-day decision-making is left to experts who are guided by data, evidence, and long-term planning. Technocratic governance can help avoid the short-termism and populism that often characterise politician-centric systems, though it also faces criticism for being undemocratic and disconnected from the will of the people.

Participatory Democracy: Expanding Citizen Involvement

Another model that seeks to move beyond politician-centric governance is participatory democracy, where citizens are more directly involved in the decision-making process. Participatory budgeting, for example, allows citizens to have a say in how public funds are allocated, giving them greater control over local governance.

By expanding opportunities for citizen participation, this model seeks to reduce the power imbalance between politicians and the public. Participatory democracy can help bridge the disconnect between rulers and the ruled, fostering a more engaged and empowered citizenry.

Decentralisation: Dispersing Power to Local Levels

Decentralisation is another strategy for addressing the limitations of politician-centric governance. By transferring authority from central governments to local or regional levels, decentralisation allows decision-making to be more responsive to the needs of local populations.

In federal systems like the United States or Germany, power is divided btween national and state governments, allowing for a more tailored approach to governance. Decentralisation can also promote innovation, as local governments experiment with new policies and solutions that may later be adopted at the national level.

The Challenges and Opportunities of Power Dynamics in Governance

The distribution of power in political systems has a profound impact on the functioning of governance. Whether in democratic or authoritarian regimes, politician-centric governance comes with inherent limitations, from corruption and self-interest to the disconnect between rulers and the public. However, by exploring alternative models of power distribution—such as technocracy, participatory democracy, and decentralisation—it is possible to address some of these limitations and create more responsive, accountable, and inclusive political systems.

Understanding the power dynamics within political systems is crucial for addressing the challenges of contemporary governance.

By analysing the strengths and weaknesses of politician-centric governance, we can begin to envision new models of power distribution that better serve the needs of the people and ensure more effective, just, and equitable governance in the future.

PART II

◆◆◆

Critique of Politician-Centric Politics

CHAPTER 4

◆◆◆

The Flaws of Representative Democracy

The philosophy of politics deals with what politics and politicians should be, but what we are dealing with is what they are; the yawning gap needs to be bridged in the interest of humanity.

In an era where democracy is considered the gold standard of governance, the cracks within representative democracy are becoming more visible. While the model offers citizens the right to vote and a voice in government, the reality often falls short of its idealistic promise. Corruption, inefficiency, and a lack of accountability plague many democracies worldwide, prompting questions about whether current systems truly serve the people.

This chapter will critically examine the flaws of representative democracy, from corruption scandals to election systems that disenfranchise voters. Using case studies from countries like the United States, Brazil, India, and Italy, we will highlight how these issues manifest and explore potential reforms to address these systemic shortcomings.

The Corruption Trap: Power, Influence, and Money

Corruption at the Core of Democracy

Representative democracy is meant to reflect the will of the people, but in practice, it is often vulnerable to corruption. Politicians, especially in countries with high campaign costs, can be swayed by wealthy donors, corporations, or lobbying groups. In return, elected officials may prioritise the interests of these groups over those of their constituents. This creates a vicious cycle where money buys political influence, and influence buys policies that further entrench wealth and power among the few.

Case Study: The United States

The United States offers a prominent example of how corruption through campaign finance can distort democracy. The *Citizens United vs. Federal Election Commission* (2010) ruling by the US Supreme Court allowed corporations and unions to spend unlimited amounts of money on political campaigns. This decision significantly amplified the influence of wealthy donors and Super PACs (Political Action Committees), which funnel enormous amounts of money into the political process.

In the 2020 election cycle, it was estimated that more than $14 billion was spent on federal elections, with much of that money coming from a small pool of wealthy donors and interest groups. This raises concerns about whether elected officials are truly representing the average voter or simply the interests of those who fund their campaigns. The revolving door between politicians and lobbying firms further exacerbates this problem. Once out of office, many politicians transition into lucrative lobbying positions, advocating for the same corporations they may have benefited while in power.

Case Study: Brazil's Operation Car Wash

Brazil's *Operação Lava Jato* (Operation Car Wash) was a sweeping investigation that exposed the depth of corruption in the country's political system. Originally an investigation into money laundering, it eventually revealed how major construction firms, like Odebrecht, funnelled millions in bribes to politicians in exchange for lucrative government contracts. This scandal implicated top officials, including former presidents, ministers, and Chief Executive Officers (CEOs), leading to widespread protests and political upheaval.

The scale of the corruption uncovered in Brazil highlighted the vulnerability of democracies where corporate interests and politics become intertwined. It showed that when politicians are beholden to private interests, public trust in democratic institutions erodes, and governance is undermined by self-interest and profit-driven decision-making.

Cronyism and Nepotism in Politics

Beyond financial corruption, cronyism and nepotism are also critical issues in representative democracies. Politicians often use their power to appoint friends, family members, or loyalists to key positions. This not only perpetuates political patronage but also undermines merit-based governance, creating inefficiencies and corruption within government institutions. Political appointments are supposed to be based on competence, but cronyism shifts the focus toward loyalty over qualifications, hurting public service effectiveness.

Case Study: Italy Under Berlusconi

Italy's political history offers a prominent example of how cronyism can undermine democracy. Silvio Berlusconi, a media mogul and three-time prime minister, repeatedly used his political power to protect his business interests and those of his allies. Throughout his political career, Berlusconi was accused of using his office to pass laws that benefited his media empire and shielded him from prosecution.

One of the most controversial instances of Berlusconi's cronyism was his appointment of close associates and media figures to senior government positions despite their lack of relevant qualifications. This erosion of meritocracy and the rise of self-serving elites within the government ultimately led to widespread dissatisfaction with Berlusconi's administration and contributed to the weakening of democratic institutions in Italy.

India is a classic case of cronyism. Dynastic politics characterises Indian politics. In Bihar state, the barely literate wife of the chief minister was catapulted from the kitchen to the cabinet and made the chief minister when her husband was sent to jail on corruption charges.

Inefficiency and Bureaucratic Stagnation

The Gridlock of Government

Representative democracy, by design, often involves slow-moving and complex processes that can lead to legislative gridlock. The need for consensus among various branches of government and across political parties can make it difficult to pass meaningful legislation. While these checks and balances are meant to prevent authoritarianism, they also contribute to inefficiency, especially in polarised political environments.

Case Study: US Government Shutdowns

In the United States, government shutdowns are a prime example of how inefficiency and gridlock can bring democratic governance to a standstill. In 2019, the US Government faced its longest shutdown in history, lasting 35 days, over a budget impasse related to President Donald Trump's demand for funding to build a border wall. The shutdown affected 800,000 federal workers, leaving them without pay and disrupting essential government services.

This political stalemate illustrated the inefficiencies that can arise when different branches of government (in this case, the executive and legislative branches) are unable to reach an agreement. It also highlighted how polarised party politics can render representative democracy ineffective in addressing urgent national concerns.

Bureaucratic Bloat: A Slow-Moving Machine

The expansion of government bureaucracies also contributes to inefficiency in representative democracies. As governments grow, so do their administrative layers, creating a complex web of agencies, departments, and regulations. While bureaucracy is essential for implementing laws and providing public services, it can also become bloated, slow, and unresponsive to the needs of citizens.

Case Study: India's Bureaucratic Delays

India, the world's largest democracy, is notorious for its labyrinthine bureaucracy. The complexity of its governmental structures often leads to significant delays in implementing policies and delivering services. In the context of rural development projects, for example, funds allocated for infrastructure development can take years to be disbursed due to bureaucratic inefficiencies and red tape. These delays hinder progress and exacerbate public frustration with the government.

One striking example is India's Mahatma Gandhi National Rural Employment Guarantee Act (MGNREGA), which aims to provide employment to rural households. While the program has been lauded for its goals, its implementation has been fraught with wage payment delays, monitoring inefficiencies, and local corruption. These issues highlight the challenge of managing large-scale social programs within an overburdened bureaucracy.

Lack of Accountability: Who Really Holds Power?

The Accountability Deficit

In theory, representative democracy holds politicians accountable through regular elections. However, in practice, elected officials are often insulated from direct accountability, especially in between election cycles. The rise of 'career politicians', who remain in office for decades, often leads to a disconnect between representatives and their constituents. When accountability mechanisms are weak, politicians can act with impunity, confident that voters have little ability to hold them responsible for their actions outside of the electoral process.

Case Study: South Africa and Jacob Zuma

South Africa's experience under former President Jacob Zuma highlights how weak accountability structures can erode democracy. Zuma, who served as president from 2009 to 2018, was repeatedly accused of corruption, particularly concerning the 'state capture' scandal, in which government resources were allegedly exploited by a wealthy family (the Guptas) with close ties to Zuma.

Despite widespread public outcry and multiple legal challenges, Zuma remained in power for nearly a decade, protected by his control over the ruling African National Congress (ANC). While Zuma eventually resigned under pressure from his party, his prolonged tenure illustrates how weak accountability mechanisms within political parties can allow politicians to act with impunity, even in the face of corruption charges.

Elite Capture: Serving the Few

One of the major critiques of representative democracy is that it can be captured by elites—whether corporate, political, or social—who wield disproportionate influence over policy decisions. Politicians may prioritise the interests of these elites over those of the general population, leading to a skewed distribution of resources and power.

Case Study: Mexico's PRI and Elite Rule

Mexico's long-dominant Institutional Revolutionary Party (PRI) was often criticised for its close ties to business elites and for fostering a system of crony capitalism. During its uninterrupted 71-year rule, the PRI effectively controlled every aspect of Mexican politics, from the executive branch to local governments. This allowed business elites and wealthy families to exert significant influence over political decisions, often to the detriment of the broader population.

The PRI's long-term rule resulted in widespread corruption and a concentration of power among elites. It also created an unresponsive political system where ordinary citizens had little say in governance. The eventual electoral defeat of the PRI in 2000 marked a turning point for Mexican democracy, but the legacy of elite capture remains a challenge in the country's political system.

Electoral Systems Favouring the Few

The Problem of Unequal Representation

The structure of electoral systems in representative democracies can often distort the will of the people. Systems such as 'first-past-the-post' (FPTP), where the candidate with the most votes wins, frequently result in governments that do not represent the majority of voters. In countries like the United Kingdom, Canada, and India, FPTP has allowed political parties to win elections and form governments with only a plurality, rather than a majority, of the popular vote.

Case Study: The United Kingdom's Electoral System

In the United Kingdom, the FPTP system has long been criticised for its tendency to distort electoral outcomes. In the 2019 general election, the Conservative Party won 43.6% of the popular vote but secured 56.2% of the seats in Parliament. Conversely, the Liberal Democrats won 11.5% of the vote but only 1.7% of the seats, demonstrating how smaller parties are often underrepresented.

This disproportionality means that millions of voters' preferences are not reflected in the composition of Parliament, leading to a sense of disenfranchisement. Electoral reform advocates have called for a shift to proportional representation, a system that would more accurately reflect the distribution of votes in Parliament, but political inertia has so far prevented meaningful change.

Voter Suppression and Gerrymandering

In some democracies, electoral systems are further undermined by practices such as voter suppression and gerrymandering. Voter suppression involves tactics that disenfranchise certain groups of voters, often minorities or lower-income citizens. Gerrymandering, the manipulation of electoral district boundaries to favour one party, is another method used to distort electoral outcomes.

Case Study: Voter Suppression in the United States

The United States has faced ongoing debates about voter suppression, particularly in states with Republican-led legislatures. In recent years, laws that require voters to show specific types of ID (identification), reduce early voting periods, and close polling stations in minority neighbourhoods have disproportionately affected African American, Latino, and low-income voters. Critics argue that these laws are designed to reduce voter turnout among groups that are more likely to vote for the Democratic Party, effectively disenfranchising millions of citizens.

Gerrymandering has also played a significant role in distorting US electoral outcomes. By manipulating district boundaries, political parties can create 'safe' districts where one party is virtually guaranteed to win, regardless of the popular vote. This practice has contributed to a polarised political landscape, where many representatives are more concerned with appeasing their party's base than with appealing to a broader electorate.

The Failure to Reflect the Popular Will

Disconnection Between Government and Citizens

One of the most fundamental flaws of representative democracy is its failure to consistently reflect the will of the people. In many cases, elected officials do not adequately represent the diverse interests of their constituents, leading to disillusionment and apathy among voters. The rise of populism and anti-establishment movements in recent years can be seen as a reaction to this perceived disconnect between governments and the people they are supposed to serve.

Case Study: France's Yellow Vest Movement

In France, the *Gilets Jaunes* (Yellow Vests) movement emerged in 2018 as a grassroots protest against the government of President Emmanuel Macron. Initially sparked by a proposed fuel tax, the movement quickly grew into a broader critique of France's political and economic system, with protesters demanding more direct representation and an end to elitism in government.

The Yellow Vest movement reflected the frustration of many French citizens, particularly those in rural areas, who felt that the government was out of touch with their needs and concerns. The movement's demands for direct democracy, including referendums on key policy issues, highlighted the growing dissatisfaction with representative democracy in France and across Europe.

Can Representative Democracy Be Reformed?

The flaws of representative democracy are becoming increasingly difficult to ignore. Corruption, inefficiency, a lack of accountability, and electoral systems that fail to reflect the popular will all undermine the legitimacy of democratic governments. As these issues continue to erode public trust, more citizens are questioning whether traditional representative models are still fit for purpose.

To address these challenges, several reforms could be implemented. Campaign finance reform, for example, could reduce the influence of money in politics, while electoral reforms such as proportional representation could ensure fairer outcomes. Strengthening accountability mechanisms, both within political parties and in government institutions, is also essential to restoring public trust in democracy.

However, these reforms will only be effective if they are accompanied by a broader cultural shift toward greater transparency, civic engagement, and political responsibility. Ultimately, the success of representative democracy depends on the willingness of citizens and politicians alike to address its flaws and work toward a system that truly represents the will of the people.

CHAPTER 5

◆◆◆

Politicians and the Influence of Power and Money

Representative democracy, in its ideal form, is meant to serve the people, where elected officials make decisions in the public interest. However, in reality, modern democracies are frequently shaped by the influence of money. Financial interests often dictate political campaigns, policy decisions, and even legislative agendas. As the cost of elections continues to skyrocket, politicians increasingly rely on wealthy donors, corporations, and special interest groups for funding. This reliance opens the door for lobbying—a process where these entities exert pressure to influence policy in their favour.

In this chapter, we will explore how financial interests, including the role of campaign finance, corporate donations, lobbying, and the revolving door between politics and business, influence politicians. Through case studies and real-world examples, we will examine the consequences of this influence, ranging from skewed policymaking to outright corruption. By analysing these dynamics, we aim to uncover the deep-seated ties between money and politics and the implications for democratic governance.

The Role of Campaign Finance in Politics

Campaign Costs and the Need for Funding

One of the most direct ways in which money influences politics is through campaign finance. Running a political campaign requires substantial financial resources for advertising, outreach, rallies, and administrative costs. In many countries, especially those with large populations or expansive media landscapes, the cost of running for office has reached astronomical levels.

Case Study: The United States – Money in Elections

In the United States, the cost of elections has risen dramatically over the past few decades. The 2020 election, for instance, was the most expensive in US history, with over $14 billion spent on federal elections alone. Much of this money comes from wealthy individuals, corporations, and special interest groups that donate through PACs and Super PACs.

One of the key events shaping the relationship between money and politics in the US was the *Citizens United vs. Federal Election Commission* ruling in 2010. The Supreme Court ruled that corporations and unions could spend unlimited amounts of money on political campaigns as long as they did not coordinate directly with candidates. This decision effectively equated financial contributions with free speech, dramatically increasing the influence of money in politics. As a result, many candidates now rely heavily on Super PACs to fund their campaigns, creating a system where political success is often tied to financial backing rather than popular support.

The Impact on Policy Agendas

The need for vast amounts of money creates a dependency on wealthy donors, who often expect something in return for their financial support. This can lead to a situation where politicians feel pressured to prioritise the interests of their donors over those of their constituents. As a result, policies that benefit corporations, wealthy individuals, or powerful industries may take precedence over policies that address the needs of ordinary citizens.

For example, the debate over healthcare reform in the United States provides a clear illustration of how campaign contributions can influence policymaking. The pharmaceutical and insurance industries are among the biggest donors to political campaigns, contributing millions of dollars to both Democratic and Republican candidates. These industries have a vested interest in preserving the status quo, which has led to resistance to significant healthcare reforms such as a single-payer system or measures to lower drug prices.

Case Study: India's Electoral Bonds and Corporate Donations

India, the world's largest democracy, faces similar challenges regarding the influence of money in politics. One of the most controversial developments in recent years has been the introduction of electoral bonds, a financial instrument that allows individuals and corporations to make anonymous donations to political parties. While proponents argue that electoral bonds provide transparency by moving donations away from cash, critics argue that the anonymity of donors encourages undue influence by wealthy corporations.

In 2019, the Association for Democratic Reforms (ADR) reported that over 90 per cent of the funds raised by major political parties in India came through electoral bonds. This has led to concerns that political parties, particularly the ruling party, are becoming increasingly dependent on corporate donations, raising questions about how these financial interests might influence government policy.

Lobbying: Shaping Policy from the Shadows

What Is Lobbying?

Lobbying is the process by which interest groups attempt to influence policymakers to enact laws or regulations favourable to their causes. Lobbying can take many forms, from direct meetings between lobbyists and legislators to more indirect strategies, such as funding think tanks, research, or public campaigns to sway public opinion. While lobbying is a legal and often necessary part of the political process, it can lead to conflicts of interest when the priorities of powerful corporations or industries outweigh the public good.

The Lobbying Industry

Lobbying has become a massive industry in many countries, with billions of dollars spent annually on influencing government policy. In the United States, for example, the lobbying industry spent $3.5 billion in 2020 alone. Corporations, trade associations, and advocacy groups hire lobbyists—many of whom are former politicians or government officials—to push their agendas in Congress, regulatory agencies, and even the White House.

Case Study: Big Pharma and Healthcare Reform in the US

The pharmaceutical industry is one of the most powerful lobbying forces in Washington, D.C. In 2020, the industry spent over $306 million on lobbying efforts, targeting both Republicans and Democrats. This spending helps explain why significant reforms to the pharmaceutical industry, such as allowing Medicare to negotiate drug prices or implementing stricter regulations on drug pricing, have been difficult to achieve despite widespread public support.

The influence of the pharmaceutical lobby was especially evident during the debates surrounding the Affordable Care Act (ACA) in 2010. While the ACA aimed to expand healthcare coverage, major pharmaceutical companies successfully lobbied to ensure that the legislation would not include provisions that would significantly lower drug prices. In exchange for their support, pharmaceutical companies reportedly agreed to provide discounted drugs to low-income Americans, but the law stopped short of more substantial reforms that would have threatened the industry's profits.

Case Study: The NRA and Gun Control Legislation

Another powerful lobbying group in the US is the National Rifle Association (NRA), which has long been a vocal advocate for gun rights. The NRA spends millions of dollars each year lobbying against gun control measures, often using its political influence to block or water down legislation aimed at curbing gun violence.

Despite multiple mass shootings in the US and growing public support for stricter gun laws, the NRA's lobbying efforts have successfully stalled significant reforms. For example, after the 2012 Sandy Hook Elementary School shooting, which killed 20 children and six adults, the US Senate failed to pass even modest gun control measures, such as expanded background checks, largely due to pressure from the NRA.

The Revolving Door: From Public Office to Private Interests

What Is the Revolving Door?

The 'revolving door' refers to the phenomenon where individuals move between roles in government and positions in the private sector, particularly in industries that they previously regulated or legislated for. This practice raises concerns about conflicts of interest, as former politicians and government officials may use their inside knowledge and connections to benefit private interests rather than serving the public good.

Case Study: The Financial Sector and Regulatory Capture

The revolving door between the financial sector and government is especially prominent, particularly in countries like the United States. Many high-ranking officials in the US Treasury Department and Federal Reserve have previously worked for major financial institutions like Goldman Sachs, JPMorgan Chase, or Citigroup. After leaving public office, many return to the private sector, where they can command high salaries for their connections and influence.

This revolving door has contributed to what is known as 'regulatory capture', a situation where government agencies tasked with regulating an industry become dominated by the very industries they are supposed to oversee. One example of this dynamic occurred in the lead-up to the 2008 financial crisis. Many former financial industry executives held key positions in the US Government, where they were responsible for regulating the banking and investment sectors. Critics argue that their close ties to Wall Street contributed to a lack of oversight and the eventual collapse of the financial system.

Case Study: Energy and Environmental Regulation

The energy sector is another area where the revolving door has had a significant impact. In the US, the Environmental Protection Agency (EPA) has faced criticism for being influenced by individuals with ties to the fossil fuel industry. During the Trump administration, several key figures within the EPA, including its Administrator Scott Pruitt, were closely aligned with the oil and gas industries. Pruitt had previously sued the EPA multiple times on behalf of the fossil fuel industry while serving as Attorney General of Oklahoma.

This close relationship between regulators and the industry led to a series of rollbacks of environmental protections, including the weakening of regulations on greenhouse gas emissions and the deregulation of public lands for oil and gas drilling. Critics argue that these policies were influenced more by the interests of the fossil fuel industry than by concerns about climate change or public health.

The Impact of Financial Influence on Policy Outcomes

Tax Policy and Wealth Inequality

One of the most significant ways in which financial interests shape policymaking is through tax policy. Wealthy individuals and corporations often lobby for tax cuts, loopholes, and exemptions that benefit them at the expense of the broader population. These efforts have contributed to rising income inequality in many countries as tax policies become increasingly skewed in favour of the rich.

Case Study: The 2017 US Tax Cuts

In 2017, the US Congress passed the Tax Cuts and Jobs Act (TCJA), which significantly reduced the corporate tax rate from 35 per cent to 21 per cent. While proponents of the law argued that the tax cuts would stimulate economic growth and create jobs, critics pointed out that the majority of the benefits would go to wealthy individuals and large corporations. Indeed, after the passage of the TCJA, many corporations used their tax savings to buy back shares and increase dividends, benefiting shareholders rather than investing in new jobs or higher wages for workers.

The TCJA also included provisions that allowed for generous deductions for certain types of income, particularly for real estate developers. Critics pointed out that these provisions appeared to be tailored to benefit individuals like then-President Donald Trump and his business empire, raising concerns about conflicts of interest and the influence of financial power on tax policy.

Environmental Policy and Corporate Influence

Another area where financial interests have a significant impact on policy is environmental regulation. Corporations in industries such as oil, gas, coal, and agriculture often lobby against environmental regulations that would increase their costs or limit their ability to operate.

Case Study: Brazil's Deforestation Crisis

In Brazil, the agricultural and mining industries have exerted significant influence over government policy, particularly under the administration of President Jair Bolsonaro. Bolsonaro has been accused of weakening environmental protections in the Amazon rainforest, allowing for increased deforestation to make way for cattle ranching, soybean farming, and mining operations. These industries are major contributors to Brazil's economy and have been major donors to Bolsonaro's political campaigns.

The consequences of these policies have been devastating for the environment, as deforestation rates in the Amazon have surged to their highest levels in over a decade. The destruction of the rainforest has not only contributed to climate change but has also led to the displacement of indigenous communities and the loss of biodiversity. Critics argue that Bolsonaro's close ties to the agricultural and mining industries have led him to prioritise short-term economic gains over long-term environmental sustainability.

Can Money Be Removed from Politics?

The relationship between politicians, power, and money is deeply entrenched in modern democracies. Financial interests shape elections, influence policymaking, and contribute to a political system that often prioritises the wealthy and powerful over ordinary citizens. While some level of financial involvement in politics may be inevitable, the current system, in which money often speaks louder than the public will, raises fundamental questions about the health of democratic governance.

Addressing the influence of money in politics will require comprehensive reforms, including campaign finance regulations, transparency in lobbying, and measures to close the revolving door between politics and private interests. However, meaningful change is unlikely to occur without significant public pressure, as those who benefit from the current system are often resistant to reform.

Ultimately, the challenge for modern democracies is to find ways to reduce the corrosive influence of money in politics while ensuring that elected officials remain accountable to the people they serve. Whether through grassroots movements, legal reforms, or shifts in political culture, the fight to curb the influence of money in politics will be central to the future of representative democracy.

CHAPTER 6

◆◆◆

Bureaucracy Vs. Politicians: Who Really Governs?

In modern democratic systems, governance is often seen as a balancing act between two key players: elected politicians, who the people choose to make laws and policy decisions, and bureaucrats, the civil servants who implement those decisions. While politicians may be the public face of government, it is often the bureaucrats who wield significant influence over how those policies are carried out. This leads to an enduring question: who really governs? Is it the elected officials who are accountable to voters or the bureaucrats who have the technical expertise and long-term institutional knowledge to navigate the complexities of governance?

This chapter explores the power dynamics between politicians and bureaucrats, the role each plays in governance, and the tension that often arises between them. We will examine how bureaucracies function, the challenges of political oversight, and case studies from different countries that highlight the competing interests of these two forces in the political system. Ultimately, this chapter seeks to uncover the nuances of governance and the often-hidden role that bureaucrats play in shaping the policies that affect everyday life.

Defining Bureaucracy and Its Role in Governance

What Is Bureaucracy?

A bureaucracy refers to a structured system of government administration composed of non-elected officials and career civil servants. Bureaucracies are typically organised into hierarchical departments, agencies, or ministries, with specialised roles and responsibilities. The purpose of a bureaucracy is to manage the daily functions of government, including implementing policies, enforcing laws, and regulating various sectors of society. Bureaucrats are expected to be neutral, professional, and efficient in their duties, relying on technical expertise and institutional knowledge to ensure that government policies are carried out effectively.

The Relationship Between Bureaucracy and Democracy

In democratic systems, bureaucrats serve under the direction of elected officials, who provide the mandate for policy direction. However, the relationship between politicians and bureaucrats is not always straightforward. Bureaucrats often possess a deep understanding of the inner workings of government, while elected officials may come and go with each election cycle. As a result, bureaucrats can exert significant influence over how policies are interpreted, implemented, and even formulated.

While politicians may have the authority to create laws and policies, bureaucrats are tasked with interpreting those laws and ensuring that they are applied in practice. This gives bureaucrats a form of power that is often hidden from the public eye but is crucial to the functioning of any government.

The Weberian Model of Bureaucracy

The German sociologist Max Weber was one of the earliest thinkers to study bureaucracy systematically. In his work, Weber identified bureaucracy as an ideal type of organisational structure characterised by hierarchy, rules, and specialisation. According to Weber, bureaucracies are essential for large organisations to function efficiently, as they provide a clear division of labour, established procedures, and a depersonalised approach to decision-making. Weber also warned, however, that bureaucracy could become overly rigid, leading to what he called the 'iron cage', where individuals are trapped by the impersonal nature of bureaucratic rules.

Politicians and Bureaucrats: A Complex Relationship

The Role of Elected Officials

Politicians, as elected representatives of the people, are responsible for making laws, setting policy agendas, and allocating resources. Their legitimacy comes from their electoral mandate, and they are expected to reflect the will of the voters. Politicians have the authority to pass laws and set the direction of government, but they often lack the time, technical expertise, or institutional memory to manage the complexities of governance on their own. This is where bureaucrats come in, as they have the specialised knowledge and experience to ensure the smooth functioning of the government.

Bureaucrats as Technocrats

Bureaucrats, on the other hand, are professionals who are typically appointed based on merit, technical skills, and expertise. Unlike politicians, who are subject to electoral pressures and public opinion, bureaucrats are insulated from the political process, allowing them to focus on the long-term functioning of government. Bureaucrats are often described as technocrats—individuals who make decisions based on technical expertise rather than political considerations.

While this insulation can be beneficial, as it allows bureaucrats to make decisions based on evidence and expertise, it can also lead to tensions with politicians, who may feel that bureaucrats are unaccountable or resistant to political directives.

Bureaucratic Discretion and the Limits of Political Oversight

Bureaucratic Discretion: Power Behind the Scenes

One of the key sources of power for bureaucrats is what is known as bureaucratic discretion—the ability to make decisions about how laws and policies are implemented. While politicians may pass laws or set policy agendas, the actual implementation of those policies is often left to bureaucrats, who have the flexibility to interpret and apply those laws in different ways.

For example, if a government passes a law to increase environmental protections, it is up to bureaucratic agencies to determine how that law will be enforced, which industries will be regulated, and what penalties will be applied for violations. This gives bureaucrats significant power to shape the practical effects of legislation, even if they are not the ones who wrote or passed the law.

The Challenges of Political Oversight

While politicians are meant to oversee the work of bureaucrats, there are often challenges in maintaining effective oversight. One issue is the sheer complexity of government operations, which can make it difficult for elected officials to fully understand what bureaucrats are doing or how policies are being implemented. Additionally, because bureaucrats often have specialised knowledge, they may be able to resist or undermine political directives by citing technical or legal justifications for their actions.

Case Study: The Brexit Negotiations and the UK Civil Service

The United Kingdom's experience with Brexit provides a clear example of the tensions between politicians and bureaucrats. After the 2016 referendum in which British voters chose to leave the European Union, it was up to the UK Government to negotiate the terms of the exit. While politicians, particularly those in favour of Brexit, set the overall direction of the negotiations, it was the civil service—specifically, the UK's Department for Exiting the European Union (DExEU)—that was responsible for managing the complex technical details of the negotiation process.

Throughout the negotiations, there were significant tensions between pro-Brexit politicians and the civil service, with some politicians accusing civil servants of being biased against Brexit or deliberately obstructing the process. For their part, civil servants argued that they were simply trying to navigate the technical and legal complexities of Brexit to achieve the best possible outcome for the UK.

This case highlights the difficulties that can arise when politicians set ambitious political goals without fully considering the practical challenges of implementation. It also demonstrates the power that bureaucrats have to shape policy outcomes, particularly in complex and technical areas like international negotiations.

Bureaucratic Power and the Deep State Debate

The Concept of the 'Deep State'

In recent years, there has been a growing public debate about the idea of a 'deep state'—a term used to describe a supposed shadow government composed of unelected bureaucrats, military officials, and intelligence agencies that operate independently of elected officials and work to undermine their policies. The term has gained particular prominence in countries like the United States and Turkey, where political leaders have accused bureaucrats and civil servants of actively working against their agendas.

While the notion of a deep state is often dismissed as a conspiracy theory, it does reflect real concerns about the power that bureaucrats and civil servants can wield behind the scenes. Bureaucrats, by their expertise and long tenure, often have a significant amount of autonomy in their decision-making, which can sometimes put them at odds with elected officials.

The Limits of Bureaucratic Accountability

One of the key criticisms of bureaucracies is that they are often perceived as being unaccountable to the public. Unlike politicians, who must stand for election, bureaucrats are appointed and can remain in their positions for decades. This long-term tenure, combined with the complexity of government operations, can make it difficult for citizens or elected officials to hold bureaucrats accountable for their actions.

Case Study: The Turkish Government and the 'Deep State'

In Turkey, the idea of the deep state has been a central theme in political discourse for decades. The term 'deep state' originally referred to a group of military and intelligence officials who allegedly operated behind the scenes to protect the secular nature of the Turkish state, often undermining elected officials who were seen as too sympathetic to Islamist or Kurdish interests.

In recent years, Turkish President Recep Tayyip Erdoğan has used the concept of the deep state to describe bureaucrats and military officials whom he accuses of conspiring to undermine his government. In response to a failed coup attempt in 2016, Erdoğan launched a massive purge of the civil service, judiciary, and military, accusing tens of thousands of bureaucrats of being part of a deep state conspiracy to overthrow him.

While Erdoğan's actions have been criticised as an authoritarian crackdown on political dissent, they also highlight the real tensions that can exist between politicians and bureaucrats, particularly in countries with a history of military intervention in politics.

Case Study: The Indian Bureaucracy and Politician Dynamics

India's Bureaucratic Structure

India's bureaucracy is one of the largest and most complex in the world, with a sprawling system of national, state, and local administrative agencies. At the heart of the system is the Indian Administrative Service (IAS), a prestigious cadre of civil servants who are responsible for managing the day-to-day operations of government at all levels.

The Indian bureaucracy has a long tradition of neutrality and professionalism, but it has also been criticised for being slow, inefficient, and resistant to reform. Bureaucrats in India often wield significant power, particularly at the state and local levels, where they are responsible for implementing government programmes and managing public resources.

Tensions Between Politicians and Bureaucrats

In India, the relationship between politicians and bureaucrats is often marked by tension. Politicians, particularly at the state level, may seek to use their authority to influence the actions of bureaucrats, while bureaucrats may resist political pressure to maintain their professional independence.

For example, in 2017, the Chief Minister of Delhi, Arvind Kejriwal, accused the bureaucracy of deliberately obstructing his government's policies. Kejriwal's government had clashed with bureaucrats over a range of issues, including healthcare, education, and anti-corruption measures. The standoff between the Delhi

Government and the bureaucracy highlighted the broader tensions between elected officials and civil servants in India, particularly in a federal system where authority is divided between different levels of government.

Yes, Prime Minister – The Complexity of Government

Government is characterised by complex dynamics of the tangibles and the intangibles; some are visible to the public, but most are not. 'Yes, Minister' and its sequel 'Yes, Prime Minister', a British political satire TV series, explores the complexity of these dynamics through ten key themes:

Bureaucracy Vs. Politics: Highlights the struggle between elected officials and career civil servants, each pushing their own agenda. In the case of India, the state of affairs in the capital city of Delhi amply highlights this aspect.

Government Inertia: Shows the difficulty of enacting change due to bureaucratic resistance.

Political Manoeuvring: Depicts the strategies politicians use to navigate their careers.

The Power of Words: Illustrates how ambiguous language can obscure truth and serve political ends. Politicians never do or say anything controversial; they are always quoted out of context as part of a political conspiracy!

Ethical Dilemmas: Presents moral challenges in governance, often resolved by prioritising pragmatism over ethics—political expediency. Someone rightly said that politics makes for strange bedfellows.

Public Image Vs. Reality: Exposes the gap between the public-facing image of government and the behind-the-scenes reality, an aspect highlighted in the book as rhetoric vs. reality.

Ministerial Responsibility: Examines accountability and the shifting of blame within government ranks.

Conflict of Interests: Shows officials balancing public duty against personal and departmental goals.

Spin and Media Manipulation: Demonstrates how information is managed to maintain political advantage. Social media is the latest tool of information and misinformation management.

Humour in Seriousness: Through satire, it reveals the absurdity of bureaucratic processes and political strategies. We have a full chapter on the absurdity of Indian politics.

These themes offer a comedic yet incisive critique of the intricacies and power plays within political and bureaucratic systems.

The Path Forward: Balancing Political Authority and Bureaucratic Expertise

Reforming Bureaucratic Oversight

The tension between bureaucrats and politicians is an inherent feature of modern governance, but some steps can be taken to improve the relationship between these two key players. One potential solution is to strengthen mechanisms of accountability for bureaucrats while also ensuring that they have the independence and resources needed to carry out their duties effectively.

Reforms aimed at increasing transparency in government operations, such as open data initiatives and stronger whistleblower protections, can help to ensure that bureaucrats are held accountable for their actions. At the same time, politicians need to recognise the value of bureaucratic expertise and avoid undermining civil servants for short-term political gain.

Building Collaborative Governance

One of the most promising approaches to resolving the tension between politicians and bureaucrats is to build a culture of collaborative governance. This involves fostering a partnership between elected officials and civil servants, where both sides work together to achieve common goals. Collaborative governance requires mutual respect, clear communication, and a shared commitment to serving the public interest.

In countries like Denmark and Sweden, which are known for their high levels of bureaucratic professionalism and political accountability, collaborative governance has been key to maintaining effective and responsive government institutions. These countries have developed a system where politicians and bureaucrats work closely together, with clear lines of responsibility and a strong emphasis on evidence-based policymaking.

Who Really Governs?

The question of who really governs—politicians or bureaucrats—is not easily answered, as both play crucial roles in the functioning of modern governments. Politicians provide the democratic legitimacy needed to set the policy agenda, while bureaucrats bring the technical expertise and institutional knowledge needed to implement those policies effectively.

However, the tension between these two forces is unlikely to disappear. As long as bureaucrats remain essential to the functioning of government, there will be debates over their accountability and the proper balance of power between elected officials and civil servants. At the same time, the rise of technocratic governance and the increasing complexity of government functions suggest that bureaucrats will continue to wield significant influence over the decisions that shape society.

The key challenge for modern democracies is to find ways to balance political authority and bureaucratic expertise, ensuring that both politicians and bureaucrats are working in the public interest. Whether through reforms that enhance accountability, promote transparency, or foster collaboration, the future of governance will depend on finding a way to harmonise the competing interests of these two pillars of the state.

PART III

◆◆◆

Rethinking Politics Without Politicians

CHAPTER 7

◆◆◆

Direct Democracy – A Step Forward?

'From Alpine Heights to Britain's shore, The common will doth rise and soar, In ballots cast, the people's lore decrees what fate may hold in store. To Kiwi lands, where choice doth reign, 'cross Latin realms, the same refrain, The globe a stage, each act in train,where vox populi sustains its domain.'

—Captain Sanjay Gahlot, co-author

In a world where politics is often seen as the domain of professional politicians, the idea of direct democracy offers an alternative: a system in which the people themselves, not elected officials, are directly responsible for making critical decisions. This approach to governance has existed in various forms throughout history, from the ancient Athenian city-states to modern-day Switzerland. Yet, in our globally interconnected and digitally empowered age, the question arises—can direct democracy be a viable model for future governance? Can we trust the populace to make informed decisions on issues as complex as economic policies, foreign affairs, or constitutional amendments? This chapter delves into the mechanics of direct democracy, examining its merits and flaws through historical examples, contemporary case studies, and theoretical reflections.

Direct democracy is defined by the absence of intermediaries, like elected representatives, in the decision-making process. Citizens vote directly on laws, policies, and initiatives, thereby exercising sovereignty without relying on an elected body to act on their behalf. As appealing as this may sound, it is important to understand how direct democracy functions, what makes it work in some places but not in others, and what challenges it presents when scaled to larger, more complex societies.

Theoretical Foundations of Direct Democracy

The theoretical roots of direct democracy can be traced back to the political philosophies of thinkers like Jean-Jacques Rousseau, who believed that the 'general will' of the people is the true source of political legitimacy. Rousseau famously wrote in *The Social Contract*, 'The moment a people gives itself representatives, it is no longer free.' For Rousseau, true democracy required citizens to be directly involved in the governance process.

However, not all political philosophers agreed with this model. Critics such as James Madison, one of the Founding Fathers of the United States, warned of the dangers of direct democracy, fearing it could lead to a 'tyranny of the majority' where minority rights would be trampled under the weight of popular opinion. Madison's solution was a representative democracy, where elected officials act on behalf of the people, ensuring that decisions are made by those equipped with the knowledge and experience to govern effectively.

In recent years, the rise of digital technology has led some political theorists to revisit Rousseau's vision. Could modern technology, with its capacity to connect millions of people and provide them with information, make direct democracy feasible on a large scale? As we explore real-world applications, we'll see how these theories have translated into practice—and where they've fallen short.

Forms of Direct Democracy

Direct democracy manifests in different forms, including referendums, citizen initiatives, recall elections, and town hall meetings. These mechanisms, while varying in scope and function, all share a common goal: enabling citizens to have a direct say in government decisions.

Referendums and Plebiscites

Referendums are perhaps the most recognisable form of direct democracy, allowing citizens to vote on specific policy questions. This process can range from decisions on local issues, such as zoning laws, to national referendums on constitutional amendments.

Brexit (2016): One of the most high-profile referendums in recent history was the United Kingdom's decision to leave the European Union. The 'Brexit' referendum saw 51.9 per cent of voters choose to exit the EU. The referendum was lauded by proponents of direct democracy as a demonstration of the people's will. However, it also highlighted significant weaknesses in the process. Many critics argued that voters were ill-informed about the complexities of leaving the EU and were swayed by populist rhetoric rather than facts. The aftermath of the vote has been marked by economic uncertainty and political chaos, raising questions about whether referendums on such complicated issues are appropriate.

Swiss Referendums: Switzerland, often held up as the gold standard for direct democracy, offers a stark contrast to the chaos of Brexit. Swiss citizens regularly vote on a wide range of issues through referendums, from healthcare reform to immigration. One of the notable features of Swiss direct democracy is the requirement for a double majority in certain cases—both the majority of voters and the majority of cantons must approve an initiative for it to pass. This system ensures a balance between popular will and regional representation, addressing some of the concerns about the tyranny of the majority.

Citizen Initiatives

Citizen initiatives allow the public to propose new laws or constitutional amendments directly, bypassing the legislature. This gives citizens more control over the political agenda, ensuring that issues important to them can be addressed even if politicians are unwilling to act.

California's Proposition 13 (1978): One of the most famous examples of a citizen initiative is California's Proposition 13, which significantly reduced property taxes and imposed restrictions on future tax increases. The proposition was immensely popular at the time and passed with 65 per cent of the vote. However, the long-term effects have been more controversial. While homeowners benefited from lower taxes, the state has struggled with underfunded public services, particularly in education and infrastructure. Proposition 13 serves as a cautionary tale about the unintended consequences of citizen initiatives, where short-term benefits can lead to long-term problems.

The European Citizens' Initiative: The EU introduced the European Citizens' Initiative (ECI) in 2012, allowing EU citizens to propose legislation. While the ECI is a novel idea, its practical impact has been limited. Proposals must garner one million signatures from at least seven member states, and even if successful, the European Commission is not obligated to act on them. This example highlights both the promise and the limitations of citizen initiatives at the supranational level.

Recall Elections

Recall elections allow voters to remove elected officials from office before the end of their term. This mechanism is seen as a way to ensure accountability, giving citizens the power to hold their leaders to account between regular elections.

California's Recall Election (2003): In 2003, California held a recall election that resulted in the removal of Governor Gray Davis and the election of actor Arnold Schwarzenegger as his replacement. The recall election, initiated by a petition from citizens unhappy with Davis's handling of the state budget, highlighted the volatile nature of direct democracy. While proponents argued that it was a necessary check on Davis's poor governance, critics warned that recall elections could be exploited by political opportunists, destabilising governance.

Town Hall Meetings

Town hall meetings offer a more informal form of direct democracy, providing citizens with the opportunity to meet face-to-face with politicians, ask questions, and express their views.

New England Town Meetings: In the United States, town meetings in New England represent one of the oldest forms of direct democracy. These annual gatherings allow residents to vote directly on local budgets and other community issues. While this model works well in small, homogenous communities, its scalability to larger, more diverse societies is questionable. Critics argue that it can lead to decisions being dominated by a vocal minority, while others praise it as a model of civic engagement.

Advantages of Direct Democracy

Direct democracy offers several benefits, particularly in terms of increasing citizen participation and ensuring accountability.

Increased Citizen Participation

One of the primary advantages of direct democracy is that it encourages active political participation. When citizens have a direct say in decision-making, they are more likely to engage with the political process and take ownership of the outcomes.

Switzerland's High Participation Rates: Switzerland's use of referendums has resulted in high levels of political engagement. Swiss citizens vote several times a year on a wide range of issues, from national policies to local matters. This frequent participation has fostered a strong civic culture, with citizens more informed and involved in their governance than in many representative democracies.

Accountability and Transparency

In direct democracy, there is a direct link between decision-makers (the citizens) and decisions. This transparency reduces the risk of corruption, as policies are not made behind closed doors by politicians beholden to lobbyists or special interest groups.

Iceland's Crowdsourced Constitution (2009): After the 2008 financial crisis, Iceland embarked on an ambitious project to rewrite its constitution with input from ordinary citizens. The process involved a mix of online platforms, town hall meetings, and referendums, allowing citizens to have a say in the country's future. While the draft constitution was ultimately blocked by the political elite, the process itself was praised for its transparency and citizen involvement.

Reduction of Corruption

By reducing the role of career politicians, direct democracy can limit opportunities for corruption. Without a small group of elected officials making decisions, there are fewer opportunities for bribery, influence-peddling, and other forms of corruption.

Switzerland's Decentralised Model: Switzerland's decentralised political system, in which citizens regularly vote on issues at the national, cantonal, and local levels, has helped keep corruption relatively low. With decision-making power spread across the population, it is more difficult for any one individual or group to exert undue influence over the process.

Challenges and Criticisms of Direct Democracy

While direct democracy offers many advantages, it is not without its challenges. Critics point to the complexity of issues, the risks of manipulation, the tyranny of the majority, and voter fatigue as significant drawbacks.

Complexity of Issues

Many of the issues faced by modern governments, such as healthcare reform, climate change, and foreign policy, are highly complex and require expert knowledge to fully understand. Asking ordinary citizens to make decisions on such matters can result in uninformed choices, leading to negative consequences.

Brexit (2016): The Brexit referendum is a prime example of how complex issues can be oversimplified in a direct democracy. Many voters admitted they didn't fully understand the implications of leaving the EU, and the referendum campaign was marked by misinformation. The decision to leave the EU has had far-reaching economic and political consequences that were not fully understood by the electorate at the time of the vote.

Manipulation and Populism

Direct democracy can be vulnerable to manipulation by charismatic leaders or populist movements that appeal to emotions rather than reason. Populist leaders may exploit direct democracy to push through policies that are popular in the short term but harmful in the long run.

Venezuela's 1999 Constitutional Referendum: In 1999, Venezuelan President Hugo Chávez used a referendum to push through a new constitution that consolidated his power. While the referendum was presented as a way to empower the people, it ultimately weakened democratic institutions and paved the way for Chávez's authoritarian rule. This example illustrates how direct democracy can be exploited by leaders seeking to entrench their own power.

Tyranny of the Majority

One of the most significant concerns about direct democracy is the risk of the 'tyranny of the majority', where the majority imposes its will on minority groups, leading to the marginalisation of those who are less politically powerful.

California Proposition 8 (2008): In 2008, California voters passed Proposition 8, a referendum that banned same-sex marriage. The proposition was later overturned by the courts, but the episode highlighted how direct democracy could sometimes lead to the erosion of individual rights, particularly for marginalised groups. The case raises questions about whether certain rights should be subject to popular vote.

Voter Apathy and Low Turnout

Frequent referendums and initiatives can lead to voter fatigue, where citizens become overwhelmed by the constant demand for their input and disengage from the political process. Low voter turnout can undermine the legitimacy of direct democratic decisions.

Swiss Referendums: While Switzerland's system of direct democracy is often praised, it also suffers from relatively low voter turnout, particularly on more technical issues. In some cases, fewer than 50 per cent of eligible voters participate, raising concerns about whether these decisions truly reflect the will of the people.

Technological Innovations in Direct Democracy

In recent years, technological innovations have offered new possibilities for enhancing direct democracy. Digital platforms, blockchain technology, and online deliberative platforms have the potential to make direct democracy more accessible, secure, and informed.

Digital Platforms for Voting

One of the most significant barriers to direct democracy is the logistical challenge of holding frequent votes. Digital platforms for voting offer a solution, making it easier for citizens to participate in decision-making from the comfort of their homes.

Estonia's e-Democracy: Estonia is a pioneer in e-democracy, offering online voting for national elections since 2005. The system allows citizens to vote securely from their computers, increasing participation and making direct democracy more feasible. While the system has been praised for its efficiency, concerns remain about security and the potential for hacking.

Blockchain Technology and Transparent Voting

Blockchain technology offers the potential for transparent and tamper-proof voting systems. By recording votes on a public, decentralised ledger, blockchain could ensure that direct democratic decisions are secure and transparent.

Potential for 'Smart Contracts': Blockchain could also facilitate the use of 'smart contracts' in governance, where citizens vote on predefined rules that automatically execute policy decisions without the need for intermediaries. This could streamline the decision-making process and reduce opportunities for corruption.

Online Deliberative Platforms

One of the key challenges of direct democracy is ensuring that citizens are informed about the issues they are voting on. Online deliberative platforms offer a solution, providing spaces for citizens to engage in meaningful discussions with experts and each other before casting their votes.

Taiwan's 'Taiwan Vs. Taiwan' Platform: Taiwan has developed an innovative online deliberative platform called Taiwan vs. Taiwan, where citizens collaborate with government officials to discuss and shape public policies. The platform has been used to address issues such as Uber's regulation and online alcohol sales. By combining deliberative democracy with direct democracy, Taiwan offers a model for how technology can enhance citizen participation and informed decision-making.

Case Studies: Successes and Failures

To understand the full potential and limitations of direct democracy, it is essential to examine real-world case studies that highlight both its successes and failures.

Switzerland: The Gold Standard of Direct Democracy

Switzerland is often cited as the most successful example of direct democracy in practice. Swiss citizens regularly vote on a wide range of issues, from national policies to local matters, and the system is credited with fostering political stability, social cohesion, and high levels of civic engagement.

Successes: Switzerland's system has allowed citizens to have a direct say in their governance, leading to a strong sense of ownership and accountability. The frequent use of referendums ensures that the government remains responsive to the will of the people, and the system's checks and balances prevent hasty decision-making.

Failures: However, the system is not without its drawbacks. Critics argue that Switzerland's cautious approach to change, driven by frequent referendums, can lead to policy stagnation. Additionally, voter turnout is often low, particularly on technical issues, raising concerns about the representativeness of the outcomes.

California: The Perils of Overuse

California's initiative and referendum system allows citizens to bypass the state legislature and propose new laws directly. While this system has led to significant progressive reforms, it has also created long-term governance challenges.

Successes: The system has empowered citizens to push for reforms that politicians were unwilling to address, such as environmental protections and criminal justice reform.

Failures: However, the frequent use of initiatives has also resulted in a patchwork of contradictory laws that make governing the state more difficult. For example, Proposition 13, which capped property taxes, has been blamed for underfunding public services, while Proposition 8 highlighted the risks of using referendums to decide on individual rights.

Iceland: The Constitution That Never Was

After the 2008 financial crisis, Iceland attempted to rewrite its constitution through a crowdsourcing process, allowing ordinary citizens to contribute to the drafting of a new constitution. The process was hailed as a model of transparency and citizen engagement.

Successes: The crowdsourced constitution was widely praised for its innovative approach and inclusion of ideas from ordinary citizens. It addressed issues such as environmental protection, human rights, and democratic reforms.

Failures: Despite the initial enthusiasm, the new constitution was ultimately blocked by political elites, highlighting the limitations of direct democracy when it comes up against entrenched political interests.

Venezuela: A Cautionary Tale

Venezuela's experience with direct democracy under Hugo Chávez offers a cautionary tale about how referendums can be manipulated by authoritarian leaders to consolidate power.

Successes: Chávez used direct democracy to push through a new constitution in 1999, which was initially seen as a way to empower the people and address social inequalities.

Failures: However, the new constitution also granted Chávez sweeping powers, allowing him to extend his term limits and weaken democratic institutions. This example highlights the dangers of populism in direct democracy, where leaders can exploit the process to entrench their own power.

Can Direct Democracy Work on a Larger Scale?

One of the most significant questions about direct democracy is whether it can work on a larger scale, particularly in diverse, populous nations like the United States or India.

Scalability Issues: Direct democracy works well in small, homogenous societies like Switzerland, but scaling it to larger, more diverse nations presents significant challenges. Issues such as voter fatigue, the complexity of national issues, and the risk of populism all become more pronounced in larger systems.

Hybrid Models: One potential solution is to combine direct democracy with representative democracy to create a hybrid system. For example, citizen assemblies could be used to complement representative democracy, ensuring that citizens have a direct say in key issues without overwhelming them with constant referendums.

The Future of Direct Democracy

As we move further into the digital age, the possibilities for direct democracy are expanding. Technology offers new ways to engage citizens, make voting more accessible, and ensure that decisions are informed and transparent.

Direct Democracy in the Digital Age: Digital platforms, blockchain technology, and online deliberative platforms all offer promising avenues for enhancing direct democracy. However, challenges remain, particularly in terms of ensuring that citizens are informed and that minority rights are protected.

Challenges to Overcome: To make direct democracy a viable alternative to representative systems, we need to address issues such as voter fatigue, the risk of populism, and the complexity of modern governance. Additionally, we must ensure that direct democracy does not lead to the erosion of minority rights or the rise of authoritarianism.

A Step Forward?

While direct democracy offers many advantages, it is not without its risks. In many cases, a hybrid model that combines direct and representative democracy may be the best way forward, ensuring that citizens have a direct say in their governance while benefiting from the expertise and stability provided by elected representatives.

Rethinking Governance

Direct democracy presents both opportunities and challenges for modern governance. While it offers the potential for increased citizen participation, accountability, and transparency, it also carries risks such as the tyranny of the majority, voter fatigue, and the manipulation of public opinion. As we consider the future of democracy, it is crucial to ensure that whatever system we adopt, whether direct, representative, or a hybrid model, promotes the core values of democracy—participation, accountability, and fairness. Only by doing so can we ensure that democracy remains a system that serves the people rather than one that is exploited by a select few.

CHAPTER 8

◆◆◆

Technocracy – Rule by Experts

In a time when global challenges grow increasingly complex and governance more cumbersome, technocracy—the notion of governance by experts—has started to re-emerge as an alluring alternative to traditional political systems. With crises like climate change, pandemics, and economic instability, the idea that experts, rather than ideologically driven politicians, should run governments is gaining momentum.

Technocracy seeks to place decision-making in the hands of those with the technical knowledge required to solve complex problems. Instead of politicians who must pander to voters, technocrats make choices based on data, facts, and rational analysis. But does such a system offer a better governance model, or does it sacrifice democratic representation and accountability? In this chapter, we explore whether technocracy could replace politicians, analyse real-world applications of technocratic governance, and assess both its advantages and criticisms.

The Origins and Theoretical Foundations of Technocracy

Technocracy's intellectual roots can be traced back to the early twentieth century, during the height of industrialisation and the birth of the scientific management movement. It arose from the growing belief in the power of science, technology, and data to improve efficiency and solve societal problems. In the eyes of early technocrats like American economist Thorstein Veblen and engineer Howard Scott, governance could be improved by removing politicians and empowering engineers, economists, and scientists to manage society based on their technical expertise.

Technocracy rejects the notion that political ideology and partisanship should guide governance. Instead, it embraces the idea that experts are better equipped to handle the complex issues that dominate today's policy landscape. Whether in urban planning, climate science, or economic policy, technocrats aim to find the most efficient solutions to problems, leveraging data and research rather than catering to popular opinion.

Key Principles of Technocracy

The key principles of technocracy are:

Rule by Experts: Governance is managed by specialists, such as scientists, engineers, or economists, who possess the necessary expertise.

Data-Driven Decision-Making: Policy decisions should be based on empirical data, scientific research, and expert consensus rather than political ideologies or public opinion.

Efficiency and Rationality: Technocracy seeks to optimise governance by focusing on long-term planning and efficient solutions, avoiding the short-term thinking that often characterises democratic electoral cycles.

Meritocracy: Power is granted based on merit and proven competence, not on popularity, wealth, or political connections.

At its core, technocracy promises rational, objective governance in a world often dominated by populism and political grandstanding. However, it also faces criticism, particularly when it comes to democratic legitimacy and the question of accountability.

Technocracy Vs. Democracy: A Clash of Values?

The rise of technocracy presents an inherent challenge to the democratic ideals that dominate modern governance. At its most basic level, democracy is about representation—elected officials are chosen to represent the will of the people. In contrast, technocracy argues that decision-making should be left to experts who are more capable of addressing complex issues. This tension creates an inevitable conflict between the values of expertise and popular representation.

The heart of this debate can be distilled into one question: Is it better for decisions to be made by those who know best or by those who represent the will of the people? Critics of technocracy argue that it subverts democratic principles, allowing unelected elites to wield power without accountability. Conversely, proponents counter that democracy often results in suboptimal policy decisions driven by emotional appeals or short-term political gains.

Central Banks and Monetary Policy: One of the most prominent examples of technocracy in action is the role of central banks in managing a country's monetary policy. Institutions like the US Federal Reserve and the European Central Bank are led by economists and financial experts who wield tremendous influence over interest rates, inflation control, and financial stability. These experts are not elected by the public, nor do they answer directly to political leaders. Instead, they are appointed based on their knowledge and expertise, making decisions based on economic data and long-term financial goals.

For instance, during the 2008 financial crisis, central banks around the world played a crucial role in stabilising the global economy. Technocrats in these institutions employed quantitative easing and other measures that were based on technical economic models rather than political considerations. However, this technocratic independence raises fundamental questions. While such policies helped stave off a deeper crisis, were these unelected officials accountable to the public for their decisions? Central banks, while praised for their steady hand during turbulent times, also contribute to growing concerns about a 'democratic deficit'.

Real-World Examples of Technocracy

While the idea of technocracy might seem abstract, it has been implemented, often in hybrid forms, in various countries around the world. From the meritocratic governance of Singapore to the role of technocrats in China's authoritarian system, these examples provide valuable insights into the successes and limitations of technocracy.

Singapore: A Technocratic Success Story

Perhaps no country has embraced technocratic governance more than Singapore. Under the leadership of Lee Kuan Yew and the People's Action Party (PAP), Singapore developed a meritocratic system that placed experts at the centre of governance. Ministers and top government officials are often drawn from the ranks of the nation's best scholars, engineers, and economists, all of whom are recruited based on their expertise rather than political connections or popular support.

Singapore's technocratic approach has produced impressive results. From being a poor, developing city-state in the 1960s, Singapore has transformed into one of the world's wealthiest nations, boasting advanced infrastructure, a strong economy, and an efficient government. Its public housing system, managed by the technocratic Housing Development Board (HDB), provides affordable, high-quality homes for the majority of its citizens, and its healthcare and education systems rank among the best globally.

However, Singapore's model also highlights the potential drawbacks of technocracy. While the government is highly efficient and competent, its technocratic governance comes at the cost of political pluralism. The PAP has dominated Singapore's political landscape since its founding, and civil liberties, including freedom of speech and assembly, are heavily restricted. Critics argue that Singapore's success is built on a form of 'benevolent authoritarianism', where technocrats make decisions that prioritise economic growth and efficiency over individual freedoms.

The big question that will be debated without end is, would you like a system that provides all the freedom but keeps the masses hungry, sick, and illiterate or a system that is 'benevolent authoritarianism' that meets all the needs of the people and the nation? That people have elected the PAP time and again in Singapore is their approval of the system in vogue.

China: A Hybrid of Technocracy and Authoritarianism

China's governance system is often described as a hybrid of technocracy and authoritarianism. While the country is led by the Communist Party, many of its top leaders are technocrats—highly educated engineers, economists, and scientists who have played a key role in the country's rapid economic development.

Technocratic Leadership: China's technocrats are responsible for crafting its five-year plans, which focus on industrial policy, infrastructure development, and technological advancement. Many of these leaders hold advanced degrees in fields like engineering and economics, and they are tasked with guiding the country through ambitious projects like the Belt and Road Initiative, renewable energy investments, and urbanisation.

The influence of technocrats has contributed to China's transformation into the world's second-largest economy. Under the leadership of these experts, China has invested heavily in infrastructure, become a global leader in renewable energy, and lifted hundreds of millions of people out of poverty.

However, China's technocratic governance is also intertwined with its authoritarian political structure, leading to concerns about human rights, censorship, and lack of accountability. The suppression of political dissent and the centralisation of power under President Xi Jinping raise important questions about the dangers of technocracy when it is not balanced by democratic oversight. While technocrats in China have driven economic growth, they operate within a system where their power is unchecked by democratic institutions.

European Union: Technocracy in Supranational Governance

The EU provides another example of technocracy in practice, particularly within its supranational institutions. The European Commission, which functions as the executive branch of the EU, is made up of appointed technocrats responsible for managing the day-to-day operations of the Union. These experts craft policies on a wide range of issues, including trade, competition, and environmental regulation.

Technocratic Governance: One of the EU's most technocratic institutions is the European Central Bank (ECB), which manages the euro and sets monetary policy for the eurozone. The ECB is tasked with maintaining price stability and managing inflation, and its decisions have profound implications for the economies of member states.

The technocratic nature of the EU's institutions allows for expertise-driven policy, particularly in complex areas like trade negotiations and financial regulation. Technocrats can make long-term decisions based on data and expert analysis without being swayed by political pressures.

However, the EU's technocratic governance has also led to accusations of a 'democratic deficit'. Citizens across the continent often feel disconnected from the decisions made by Brussels-based technocrats, whom they did not directly elect. This disconnection contributed to the rise of Euroscepticism, culminating in events like the UK's Brexit vote, where British citizens expressed frustration with their perceived lack of influence over EU governance.

Advantages of Technocracy: Technocracy offers several clear advantages, particularly in an increasingly complex world where policy decisions require specialised knowledge and expertise.

Expertise in Complex Policy Areas

One of the most significant advantages of technocracy is its ability to handle complex policy issues that require specialised knowledge. Issues such as climate change, public health, and economic regulation are often beyond the scope of ordinary citizens and elected politicians who lack technical expertise. Technocrats, however, are trained to navigate these complexities.

COVID-19 and Public Health Expertise

The COVID-19 pandemic offers a prime example of the value of technocratic governance. As the virus spread across the globe, public health experts, epidemiologists, and scientists played a central role in advising governments on how to manage the crisis. Countries that followed the advice of these experts, such as New Zealand, South Korea, and Taiwan, were able to control the spread of the virus more effectively than those where political considerations dominated.

Efficiency and Long-Term Planning

In democratic systems, politicians are often incentivised to focus on short-term concerns to win re-election. This can lead to shortsighted policies that prioritise immediate political gains over long-term planning. In contrast, technocrats are not constrained by electoral cycles and can make decisions based on what is best for the long-term health of the nation.

Singapore's Long-Term Planning

Singapore's technocratic governance has allowed it to engage in long-term planning that is rare in other countries. From the construction of its world-class Changi Airport to its investment in water security, Singapore's leaders have focused on long-term solutions to challenges that are unlikely to garner short-term political rewards. This ability to think beyond electoral cycles has contributed to the city-state's enduring success.

Reduction of Partisanship and Populism: Technocracy seeks to eliminate the influence of partisanship and populism in decision-making. By focusing on data and rational analysis, technocrats can craft policies that are grounded in evidence rather than political ideology or emotional appeals.

European Central Bank (ECB): The ECB operates independently from political influence, making decisions based on economic data rather than the whims of politicians. This independence allows the ECB to take difficult but necessary actions—such as raising interest rates to control inflation—without fear of political backlash. By insulating monetary policy from electoral pressures, the ECB exemplifies how technocratic governance can prioritise the long-term stability of the economy over short-term political gains.

Challenges and Criticisms of Technocracy

Despite its advantages, technocracy faces several criticisms, particularly regarding its democratic legitimacy and potential for authoritarianism.

Lack of Accountability: Perhaps the most significant criticism of technocracy is its lack of democratic accountability. Technocrats, by definition, are not elected by the people, which means that they are not directly accountable to the electorate. This can lead to a sense of disconnection between the governed and the governing.

The European Union's 'Democratic Deficit': The EU has often been criticised for its 'democratic deficit', particularly concerning the European Commission and the ECB. These institutions wield significant power over the lives of EU citizens, yet they are run by unelected technocrats. This lack of accountability has fuelled rising Euroscepticism, as citizens feel that decisions affecting their daily lives are being made by distant experts rather than by elected representatives.

Elitism and Technocratic Arrogance: Technocracy can foster a sense of elitism, where experts assume they know what is best for society without consulting the broader population. This can lead to a disconnect between technocrats and ordinary citizens, particularly when policy decisions seem out of touch with the realities of everyday life.

Italy's Technocratic Government Under Mario Monti: In 2011, during a financial crisis, Italy appointed Mario Monti, an economist and former European Commissioner, as prime minister to lead a technocratic government. While Monti's government was praised for its financial reforms, his austerity measures were deeply unpopular among ordinary Italians, many of whom viewed his policies as elitist and disconnected from the struggles of everyday life. This backlash against technocratic governance underscores the potential for resentment when experts impose decisions without considering the views of the public.

Risk of Authoritarianism: Without the checks and balances provided by democratic institutions, technocracy can slip into authoritarianism. While technocrats are experts, they are not immune to the dangers of concentrated power. Without democratic oversight, technocratic governance can become unaccountable, leading to abuses of power and the suppression of dissent.

China's Technocratic Authoritarianism: China's governance model is often cited as a hybrid of technocracy and authoritarianism. While China's technocrats have overseen significant economic growth, their governance is deeply intertwined with the authoritarian control of the Communist Party. The lack of democratic accountability has led to widespread censorship, human rights abuses, and the suppression of political opposition. This example highlights the dangers of technocracy when it operates without democratic safeguards.

The Future of Technocracy: Can Experts Replace Politicians?

As we look towards the future, the question remains—can technocrats truly replace politicians, or is a hybrid model more realistic? Technocracy offers clear advantages, but it must be balanced with democratic principles to ensure that governance remains accountable, transparent, and responsive to the will of the people.

Technocracy and Democracy: A Possible Hybrid?

Rather than fully replacing politicians, technocracy could function as a complement to democratic governance. In such a hybrid system, elected officials would still represent the will of the people, while technocrats would manage specific policy areas that require technical expertise.

Finland's Hybrid Model

Finland offers an example of how technocracy and democracy can work together. During the COVID-19 pandemic, Finland's government collaborated closely with public health experts to craft evidence-based policies that balanced the need for public health with democratic oversight. This hybrid approach allowed the government to make informed decisions while remaining accountable to the public.

The Role of Technology in Enhancing Technocracy

In the digital age, technology offers new possibilities for enhancing technocracy. AI, big data, and machine learning could be used to analyse vast amounts of information and provide technocrats with the tools to make more informed decisions.

Estonia's Digital Governance

Estonia has pioneered the use of digital governance, known as 'e-Estonia', to streamline public services and make the government more transparent. Estonia's digital infrastructure allows citizens to access services online, and real-time data collection helps technocrats monitor and manage public resources more efficiently.

Balancing Expertise with Representation

Ultimately, the success of technocracy depends on finding the right balance between expertise and representation. While experts are essential for managing complex issues, democratic accountability ensures that citizens have a voice in the decision-making process.

The IPCC and Climate Change

The United Nations' Intergovernmental Panel on Climate Change (IPCC) is an example of how technocracy and democracy can work together. The IPCC is composed of scientists and experts who provide evidence-based recommendations on climate policy, while governments and elected officials make the final decisions on how to implement these recommendations. This collaboration ensures that expertise guides policy while democratic institutions retain final decision-making authority.

Rethinking Governance in the Age of Complexity

In an increasingly complex world, the need for expertise in governance is undeniable. Technocracy offers a compelling vision of efficient, evidence-based decision-making, but it must be balanced with democratic principles to ensure accountability, transparency, and the protection of individual rights. Rather than fully replacing politicians, technocrats could play a complementary role in governance, working alongside elected officials to address society's most pressing challenges. In this hybrid model, the wisdom of experts would guide policy decisions, while the will of the people would remain at the heart of governance.

CHAPTER 9

◆◆◆

Decentralisation and Localised Governance

In the modern world, the inefficiencies, corruption, and unresponsiveness of centralised political systems have led to a global movement toward decentralisation. Decentralisation is the transfer of decision-making powers, responsibilities, and resources from the central government to local governments, communities, or grassroots organisations. This system aims to empower local stakeholders, making governance more responsive and accountable to the needs of local populations and authentically reflecting the local realities. This authenticity ensures that governance is not a one-size-fits-all model but a dynamic and adaptive system that evolves in response to the nuanced needs of diverse localities. The policies crafted under this paradigm resonate with the pulse of communities, fostering a sense of ownership and alignment with broader societal goals.

The chapter explores how decentralisation reduces the reliance on centralised politicians and enables localised, grassroots decision-making.

We will explore the history and theoretical framework of decentralisation, look at its different models, and examine real-world case studies. We will also delve into how decentralisation can empower local actors, improve service delivery, reduce corruption, and create more accountable and inclusive governance structures.

Theoretical Foundations and History of Decentralisation

Decentralisation is not a modern phenomenon. Historically, societies have oscillated between centralised and decentralised forms of governance, depending on the level of social complexity and geography. Decentralisation was common in feudal systems, where local lords held political and military control. In the modern world, decentralisation became an alternative model to address the challenges that come with large, centralised bureaucracies.

Key Concepts in Decentralisation

Decentralisation can be exercised in the following ways:

Subsidiarity: This principle suggests that decisions should be made at the lowest appropriate level of government. Higher levels of government should intervene only when local governments are unable to manage an issue on their own.

Autonomy: Local governments should have the legal and financial autonomy to act independently without constant interference from central authorities.

Local Participation: Decentralisation increases citizen involvement in governance by encouraging grassroots participation, ensuring that policies are reflective of local needs.

Global Shift Towards Decentralisation

The shift towards decentralisation gained traction in the twentieth century, particularly in post-colonial countries where centralisation often led to inefficiencies and exclusion. Today, decentralisation is seen as a means to enhance governance, particularly in large and diverse countries like India, Brazil, and Nigeria.

Case Study: Decentralisation in the European Union

The EU has embedded decentralisation into its structure through the principle of subsidiarity. While certain issues like trade and security are handled at the central EU level, areas like healthcare, education, and transportation are managed by individual member states and regions. This decentralised model has allowed the EU to accommodate the diversity of its 27 member states.

Models of Decentralisation: Political, Administrative, and Fiscal

Decentralisation takes many forms, depending on how powers are transferred to local bodies. It is not a one-size-fits-all solution, and different countries adopt models based on their unique challenges and governance needs.

Political Decentralisation

Political decentralisation refers to the transfer of decision-making powers to elected local officials. This model allows citizens to elect local leaders who are responsible for local governance, creating a closer relationship between voters and politicians.

The Panchayati Raj System in India is one of the most significant examples of political decentralisation. Established through the 73rd Constitutional Amendment Act in 1992, the system grants local elected bodies (panchayats) the power to manage local resources, oversee rural development, and make decisions related to education, healthcare, and infrastructure. This model has empowered local communities, particularly in rural India, reducing dependence on centralised government officials to address basic needs.

The 74th Constitutional Amendment Act sought to strengthen urban local bodies, municipalities, and municipal corporations, providing a framework for their governance. It emphasised the importance of urban local self-governance as a response to rapid urbanisation and the complex challenges of urban management.

Administrative Decentralisation

Administrative decentralisation involves the transfer of responsibilities related to public services from central to local governments. It aims to improve the efficiency and accountability of public service delivery, such as healthcare, education, and public transportation.

Colombia's Decentralised Health System

In the 1990s, Colombia implemented administrative decentralisation by giving local governments control over healthcare services. This move allowed local authorities to tailor health services to meet the specific needs of their communities, leading to significant improvements in health outcomes, particularly in rural and underserved areas. Local governments now have greater accountability in managing public hospitals, clinics, and health insurance systems.

Fiscal Decentralisation

Fiscal decentralisation gives local governments the authority to raise and spend revenues. This model allows local bodies to generate funds through taxes, ensuring that local resources are allocated in ways that directly reflect the priorities of local communities.

In Porto Alegre, Brazil, fiscal decentralisation is demonstrated through participatory budgeting. Citizens are directly involved in determining how municipal tax revenues are allocated. This process has led to increased transparency, reduced corruption, and better alignment between public spending and the needs of local communities. Projects related to education, sanitation, and infrastructure have been prioritised based on public input.

Case Studies: Success Stories in Decentralised Governance

Decentralisation has proven successful in several parts of the world. The following case studies highlight how decentralised governance has reduced the role of centralised politicians and improved local governance.

Case Study 1: Switzerland's Decentralised Federalism

Switzerland is often cited as a prime example of a decentralised federal system. With 26 cantons (states) and over 2,200 municipalities, the country's governance is highly localised. Cantons have wide-ranging powers, from setting tax rates to managing healthcare and education systems. The federal government in Bern provides oversight but intervenes only when necessary. The key benefits are:

Local Autonomy: Each canton has its constitution, parliament, and budget, allowing for policies tailored to local needs.

Direct Democracy: Swiss citizens can propose and vote on policy issues at the municipal, cantonal, and federal levels. This system diminishes the need for powerful national politicians and ensures that citizens have direct input on critical decisions.

Low Corruption and High Accountability: The decentralisation of power has led to low levels of corruption and high government transparency.

Case Study 2: Bolivia's Popular Participation Law

Bolivia introduced the Popular Participation Law in 1994, which devolved significant powers to municipal governments. Local governments gained control over education, health, and infrastructure, while citizens were encouraged to participate in local governance through community-based organisations. The outcome of the initiative was:

Empowerment of Rural and Indigenous Communities: Decentralisation has allowed marginalised rural and indigenous communities to have a say in how resources are allocated and how development projects are prioritised. This shift has reduced the reliance on national politicians to address rural development issues.

Improved Service Delivery: Municipal governments now have the autonomy to manage services like water supply, schools, and health clinics, leading to more responsive and tailored service delivery.

Case Study 3: Kenya's Devolution Post-2010 Constitution

Kenya's 2010 Constitution introduced devolution, creating 47 counties with significant autonomy over local governance. County governments are now responsible for health, agriculture, trade, and infrastructure development. It derived the following benefits:

Localised Service Delivery: Counties now manage healthcare, agriculture, and infrastructure development based on local priorities rather than relying on Nairobi to make decisions.

Increased Political Representation: Devolution has allowed previously marginalised regions like northern Kenya to have greater representation and control over their resources.

Advantages of Decentralisation

Decentralisation offers a range of advantages, particularly when it comes to reducing the need for centralised politicians and increasing local accountability.

Improving Service Delivery and Responsiveness: Decentralisation brings government closer to the people, making public services more responsive to local needs. Local governments have better knowledge of their constituents' requirements and can tailor services accordingly.

The Indian state of Kerala has implemented decentralised waste management through local panchayats and municipalities. By giving local governments the responsibility to manage waste collection and disposal, the state has improved sanitation services and reduced the burden on centralised authorities.

Enhancing Accountability and Reducing Corruption: When power is concentrated in the hands of a few central politicians, corruption can thrive. Decentralisation reduces the risk of corruption by creating multiple layers of accountability. Local governments are more visible and accessible to their constituents, making it easier for citizens to monitor how resources are used.

Uganda's decentralisation program in the 1990s was designed to reduce corruption and improve service delivery. By giving local governments greater autonomy, the program increased transparency and accountability, particularly in the management of education and healthcare services. Local governments were required to report on budget allocations, reducing the opportunities for corruption.

Empowering Local Communities and Citizens: Decentralisation encourages greater citizen participation in governance, empowering local communities to shape the policies that affect their lives. Grassroots decision-making reduces the need for top-down governance by ensuring that communities have a direct say in development priorities.

In the late 1990s, Kerala launched the People's Planning Campaign, a participatory governance initiative that involved local communities in drafting development plans. Citizens were encouraged to participate in village assemblies, where they discussed local issues and determined how public resources should be allocated. This participatory approach has reduced the need for centralised politicians to intervene in local development projects.

Challenges of Decentralisation: Coordination and Capacity Issues

While decentralisation offers numerous advantages, it also faces significant challenges. Local governments may lack the capacity to manage resources effectively, and there may be difficulties in coordinating between local and national authorities.

Lack of Capacity at the Local Level: In some countries, local governments may not have the technical expertise or financial resources to manage complex services like healthcare or infrastructure development. Decentralisation without adequate capacity-building can lead to inefficient governance.

Nigeria's Decentralisation Struggles: Nigeria's federal system grants significant autonomy to its 36 states. However, many state governments lack the capacity to manage critical sectors like education and healthcare. Corruption and mismanagement at the state level have hindered the effectiveness of decentralisation in some regions.

Coordination Between Local and Central Governments: Decentralisation requires effective coordination between local and central governments to ensure that policies are aligned and resources are distributed equitably. Without strong coordination mechanisms, decentralisation can lead to fragmented governance.

The Philippines has pursued decentralisation through its Local Government Code of 1991. While local governments have gained control over health, education, and infrastructure, there have been challenges in coordinating with central authorities. Disparities in resource allocation and inconsistent policies between local and national governments have led to inefficiencies in service delivery.

The Future of Decentralisation: Strengthening Local Governance

As countries continue to explore decentralisation as a model for governance, it is important to address the challenges and build on the successes. Strengthening local governance will require investing in capacity-building, improving coordination mechanisms, and ensuring that local governments have the financial autonomy to manage their resources effectively.

Capacity Building for Local Governments

Investing in the training and development of local government officials will be crucial for the success of decentralisation efforts. Local leaders must have the technical skills and knowledge to manage complex services like healthcare, education, and infrastructure development.

Strengthening Financial Autonomy

Fiscal decentralisation must be accompanied by financial reforms that allow local governments to generate their revenue. This will reduce their dependence on central transfers and empower them to manage local resources effectively.

Ensuring Accountability and Transparency

Decentralised governance must prioritise accountability and transparency to prevent corruption and ensure that public resources are used effectively. Citizen participation, transparency measures, and regular audits can help maintain accountability at the local level.

Decentralisation as a Path to Better Governance

Decentralisation offers a promising path toward more accountable, responsive, and efficient governance. By transferring decision-making power to local governments and communities, decentralisation reduces reliance on centralised politicians and allows citizens to take control of their governance. While challenges remain, the successes of decentralised governance in countries like Switzerland, Bolivia, and Kenya demonstrate its potential to create more inclusive and effective political systems. As governments around the world continue to experiment with decentralisation, it will be essential to address the challenges and invest in the capacity of local governments to manage their responsibilities effectively.

PART IV

◆◆◆

Political Models in Action: Case Studies and Examples

CHAPTER 10

◆◆◆

Switzerland's Model of Direct Democracy

When we think of governance, it's typically the politicians who come to mind. Elected representatives, entrenched political parties, and centralised governments seem to dominate most democratic systems across the globe. However, in the quiet, neutral country of Switzerland, the people themselves take centre stage. Switzerland's model of direct democracy allows citizens to vote directly on laws and constitutional amendments through referendums and popular initiatives, creating a system that truly lives up to the democratic ideal of governance 'by the people, for the people'.

Switzerland's democratic system provides an example of how governments can function in a decentralised, participatory way, where citizens are not only voters in elections but active participants in the policymaking process. At a time when many citizens around the world feel disenfranchised and disconnected from their governments, Switzerland offers a reminder of what participatory governance can achieve. This chapter will explore Switzerland's model of direct democracy, looking into its history, functionality, and impact through major case studies. It will also assess whether this model could be implemented in other nations and what lessons it provides in navigating modern governance challenges.

Historical Origins of Swiss Direct Democracy

The story of Swiss direct democracy begins centuries ago, with the country's unique political landscape deeply rooted in its mountainous geography and a confederation of cantons, each with distinct identities. This decentralised structure made direct citizen participation not only a possibility but a necessity.

The Early Days: Cantonal Independence and the Landsgemeinde

Direct democracy in Switzerland can be traced back to the thirteenth century when small, rural communities would gather to vote on local issues in open-air assemblies known as *Landsgemeinden*. These meetings were the earliest examples of Swiss citizens directly participating in political decision-making. Originally practised in rural cantons like Uri and Schwyz, the *Landsgemeinde* allowed eligible citizens (initially only male landowners) to gather annually, raise their hands, and vote on laws, taxes, and even elect local officials. Today, only a few cantons, namely, Appenzell Innerrhoden and Glarus, still practice this ancient form of direct democracy, but the spirit of direct citizen involvement continues to define Switzerland's political system.

The 1848 Constitution: A National Experiment in Direct Democracy

The modern Swiss political system began with the Federal Constitution of 1848, which established Switzerland as a federal state. This constitution came on the heels of internal conflicts between liberal and conservative forces. The result was a political compromise that combined elements of representative democracy with mechanisms for direct democracy. The constitution introduced the popular referendum at the national level, giving Swiss citizens the right to challenge laws passed by the federal government. It was a bold experiment in democratic governance, giving ordinary citizens unprecedented power over national decision-making.

Expansion of Popular Participation: The Evolution of Direct Democracy

In 1891, the popular initiative was introduced, allowing Swiss citizens to propose constitutional amendments. To do this, proponents needed to gather 100,000 signatures within a set period. Once enough signatures were collected, the proposal would be put to a national vote. This development made Switzerland one of the most direct democracies in the world, giving citizens not only the power to reject laws but also the ability to propose changes to the country's constitution.

The Federal Constitution Referendum of 1874

In 1874, Swiss citizens voted on a crucial revision of the Federal Constitution. This revision strengthened the central government while preserving the autonomy of the cantons, setting the stage for the modern Swiss federal system. The ability of the people to vote on such an important constitutional matter highlighted the growing power of direct democracy in Switzerland and laid the foundation for its expansion throughout the twentieth century.

How Switzerland's Direct Democracy Works

Switzerland's political system is based on a delicate balance between representative democracy and direct citizen participation. While Swiss citizens elect representatives to the federal parliament, they also maintain the power to directly influence laws and policies through referendums and initiatives. The Swiss model functions at three levels: the federal, cantonal, and municipal levels.

Popular Initiatives: Citizen-Led Constitutional Amendments

Perhaps the most famous aspect of Switzerland's direct democracy is the popular initiative. If a group of citizens wishes to amend the constitution, they can launch an initiative by gathering 100,000 signatures from eligible voters within 18 months. Once the necessary signatures are collected, the proposal is put to a nationwide vote.

The popular initiative is a powerful tool for grassroots activism. It allows citizens to bypass parliament and directly propose changes to the constitution. However, initiatives must pass a 'double majority'—a majority of voters across the country and a majority of Switzerland's 26 cantons. This ensures that amendments are not only popular nationwide but also supported by a majority of cantonal regions.

The Referendum: A Citizen's Right to Challenge Laws

In addition to popular initiatives, Switzerland's referendum system allows citizens to challenge laws passed by the federal government. If opponents of a law gather 50,000 signatures within 100 days of the law's passage, the law is suspended and put to a national vote. This mechanism provides an important check on the power of elected officials, ensuring that controversial or unpopular laws can be overturned by the people.

There are also mandatory referendums, where any proposed changes to the constitution must be approved by a national vote. This ensures that no fundamental changes to Swiss governance occur without the direct consent of the people.

Frequency and Participation: Swiss Voting Culture

Switzerland holds more referendums and initiatives than any other country in the world. Swiss citizens are called to the polls multiple times a year to vote on various local, cantonal, and national issues.

This frequent voting has fostered a culture of civic engagement, where citizens feel empowered to participate in political decision-making regularly.

Though voter turnout in Swiss referendums averages between 40 and 50 per cent, the depth of engagement is notable. Citizens are often highly informed about the issues they vote on, thanks in part to detailed government pamphlets and extensive public debates.

The Popular Initiative on Universal Basic Income (2016)

In 2016, Swiss voters were asked to decide on a radical proposal: the introduction of a Universal Basic Income (UBI) for all citizens. The initiative, which proposed giving every Swiss adult a monthly payment regardless of employment status, sparked a nationwide debate on the future of work and welfare. Although the initiative was rejected by 76.9 per cent of voters, the debate it sparked resonated far beyond Switzerland, influencing discussions on UBI in other countries.

Case Studies: Direct Democracy in Action

Switzerland's system of direct democracy has been shaped by numerous referendums and popular initiatives that have addressed a wide range of issues, from social policies to environmental protection. The following case studies highlight the power of Swiss citizens to shape their country's future directly.

Case Study 1: The 1989 Nuclear Power Moratorium

In 1989, Swiss citizens voted on a referendum to impose a ten-year moratorium on the construction of new nuclear power plants. This vote came in response to growing concerns about the safety of nuclear energy following the Chernobyl disaster in 1986. The referendum passed with 54.5 per cent of the vote, leading to a decade-long freeze on new nuclear power projects.

The moratorium forced Switzerland to reconsider its energy policy, with increased investment in renewable energy sources such as hydropower and solar energy. Although the moratorium was lifted after ten years, the 1989 vote set the stage for a longer-term public debate on the future of nuclear energy in Switzerland.

Case Study 2: The 2009 Minaret Ban

One of the most controversial votes in recent Swiss history was the 2009 referendum that proposed banning the construction of minarets on mosques. The initiative, backed by right-wing groups, argued that minarets were a symbol of political Islam and were incompatible with Swiss values. The proposal passed with 57.5 per cent of the vote, sparking widespread international criticism.

The minaret ban highlighted the tension between majority rule and minority rights in direct democracy systems. While the vote reflected the will of the majority, critics argued that it violated religious freedoms and was discriminatory against Switzerland's Muslim population.

The case also demonstrated the ability of direct democracy to amplify populist and nationalist sentiments, raising questions about how to balance citizen participation with human rights protections.

Case Study 3: The 2017 Corporate Tax Reform

In 2017, Swiss voters rejected a government proposal to reform the country's corporate tax system. The proposal aimed to bring Switzerland's tax laws in line with international standards by reducing preferential tax treatment for multinational corporations. However, critics argued that the reform would result in tax breaks for large corporations while increasing the tax burden on ordinary citizens.

The rejection of the corporate tax reform forced the government to revise its proposal and negotiate a compromise that addressed public concerns. The episode demonstrated the power of Swiss citizens to hold their government accountable for complex economic issues.

It also highlighted the importance of transparency and public trust in the political process, as the government's failure to communicate the benefits of the reform led to its rejection by the electorate.

Strengths and Challenges of Swiss Direct Democracy

While Switzerland's system of direct democracy is often praised for its inclusivity and responsiveness, it also faces significant challenges. In this section, we will explore both the strengths and limitations of the Swiss model.

Strengths of Swiss Direct Democracy

Empowerment of Citizens: Switzerland's direct democracy empowers citizens to take an active role in shaping their country's policies. Voters are not passive recipients of government decisions; they are co-creators of the political system.

High Accountability: Swiss politicians know that their decisions can be overturned by a referendum, which creates a high degree of accountability. This system encourages transparency and forces politicians to engage with the public before passing controversial laws.

Policy Stability: The requirement for a double majority in constitutional amendments ensures that policies have broad support across both the population and the cantons. This creates long-term policy stability, as laws that pass through direct democracy tend to reflect the consensus of the population.

Challenges of Swiss Direct Democracy

Voter Fatigue: One of the criticisms of Switzerland's system is that frequent voting can lead to voter fatigue, where citizens become disengaged from the process. With up to four voting sessions per year and multiple issues on the ballot, some voters may feel overwhelmed by the sheer volume of decisions they are asked to make.

Complexity of Issues: Direct democracy requires citizens to vote on a wide range of complex issues, from healthcare reform to economic policy. Critics argue that many voters may not have the expertise to make informed decisions on these topics, leading to suboptimal outcomes.

Risk of Populism: The Swiss system can amplify populist sentiments, as seen in the 2009 minaret ban. While direct democracy gives citizens a voice, it also raises questions about the balance between majority rule and the protection of minority rights.

The 2014 Immigration Referendum

In 2014, Swiss voters narrowly approved an initiative to impose immigration quotas, challenging Switzerland's bilateral agreements with the EU on the free movement of people. The vote, which passed with 50.3 per cent of the vote, created a political crisis as the Swiss Government struggled to reconcile the public's desire for immigration control with its obligations under EU treaties. This case highlights the tension between national sovereignty and international commitments in direct democracy systems.

Lessons from Switzerland: Can Direct Democracy Work Elsewhere?

Switzerland's model of direct democracy offers valuable lessons for other countries considering adopting elements of citizen participation. While the Swiss system is deeply rooted in the country's unique political and cultural context, some aspects could be adapted to fit other nations.

Tailoring Direct Democracy to Local Contexts: Countries that are considering adopting direct democracy must tailor the system to fit their unique political and cultural contexts. Switzerland's success is partly due to its long history of federalism and local autonomy, which may not be easily replicated in more centralised states.

Safeguards Against Populism and Short-Term Thinking: One of the criticisms of direct democracy is that it can lead to short-term thinking and populist decisions. Countries adopting elements of direct democracy should consider implementing safeguards, such as requiring a supermajority for constitutional amendments or limiting the frequency of votes on highly divisive issues.

Civic Education: Preparing Citizens for Direct Participation

A key factor in the success of Switzerland's direct democracy is the high level of political literacy among its citizens. For direct democracy to succeed elsewhere, governments must invest in civic education to ensure that voters have the knowledge and tools to make informed decisions. Public debates, government-issued pamphlets, and accessible information about the issues on the ballot are essential components of a successful direct democracy system.

The Promise and Perils of Swiss Direct Democracy

Switzerland's model of direct democracy offers a compelling vision of citizen participation in governance. Through referendums and initiatives, Swiss citizens are empowered to shape the laws and policies that govern their lives. However, the system also comes with challenges, including the risk of voter fatigue, the complexity of issues, and the potential for populism.

As other countries explore the possibilities of direct democracy, Switzerland provides valuable lessons on how to balance citizen participation with the complexities of modern governance. With the right safeguards and a commitment to civic education, elements of the Swiss model could be adapted to create more responsive and inclusive political systems worldwide.

CHAPTER 11

◆◆◆

Navigating Governance: Merit-Based Leadership

Are you getting the leadership you deserve? Are the best people joining politics?

> *It is a well-known fact that those people who most want to rule people are those least suited to do it... those capable of getting themselves made president should on no account be allowed to do the job....*
>
> —Douglas Adams,
> *The Restaurant at the End of the Universe*

Donald Trump was elected President for the first time with no political experience. He was indicted twice for serious issues, yet was re-elected the President of the United States (POTUS) for a second term after Joe Biden. The British PM Liz Truss lasted 45 days. Volodymyr Zelensky, President of Ukraine, is a comedian by profession. He has allowed his country to slip into a disastrous war at the behest of foreign powers because of a lack of experience. Indira Gandhi imposed an emergency in 1975 for no other reason than political expediency. She was re-elected in 1980. Nitish Kumar has taken oath nine times as chief minister of Bihar, matching the education qualification of his deputy, who was Class IX pass, switching alliances purely based on political expediency, sacrificing all ideology and ethics. Prime Minister Prachanda in Nepal has switched alliances thrice in two years to remain in power. A cursory scan shows that politics is one arena where ethics and values are routinely violated without consequences. For sure, politics makes for strange bedfellows.

Every aspiring politician must be required to answer the following questions:

- What do you want power for?
- What are your goals, and how do you plan to achieve them?
- What would cause you to step down after you achieve it?
- What should cause you to be removed from that position?
- What makes you qualified and suitable for this responsibility?
- What voluntary public service have you rendered?
- Rate yourself in integrity on a scale of 10.
- Why should people elect you as their representative?

Ever wondered why the politicians never leave by choice and keep hanging on to power until either death or elections do them part? Have you ever seen a politician say, 'My five-year tenure is over, and I must relinquish power and go back to private life?' How often have you seen a politician accept responsibility for failure or poor performance?

Democracy is great, so everyone says. After the Doctor Abhaya rape and brutal murder case in RG Kar Medical College in August 2024 and the dirty dance of politics that unfolded in Bengal, do you still believe so? Are we really happy with the system that exists today, or can it be improved to get the best to govern, or at the least keep the bad apples out? Ever wondered why General KM Cariappa, an outstanding army chief, TN Seshan, the upright civil servant, and E Sreedharan, India's brilliant Metro Man, lost elections? A criminal politician has a far greater chance of being elected than an honest one.

Look around you, and you will largely agree with us.

Why do good people not want to be politicians? Why do good people not get elected as politicians?

Thus, we need to seek and recruit people with proven character and leadership credentials who do not want to be politicians, for people who are looking for political power are the least worthy of that position. We need people who have delivered selfless social service. The people who don't want power are the ones most worthy of giving power.

The Merits and Drawbacks of Merit-Based Leadership

In the dynamic realm of governance, the paradigm of merit-based leadership has emerged as a compelling force, finding expression in models such as technocratic governments and councils of experts. This approach, grounded in the principles of competence, expertise, and meritocracy, stands at the intersection of proficiency and the weighty responsibilities that leadership demands. As we embark on a journey into the intricacies of these models, a nuanced debate unfolds, illuminating the multifaceted terrain where the virtues of proficiency encounter the challenges inherent in leadership roles.

Merit-based leadership in politics refers to a system where individuals are selected for leadership positions based on their qualifications, skills, and abilities, rather than political connections or personal relationships.[1] The merit system principles provide a framework for responsible behaviour and are key to mission success.[2] The principles include open competition, fairness, and the recognition of better performance.[3] Navigating the intersection of politics and leadership requires a balance of strategic thinking, effective communication, and a willingness to collaborate.[4] It is important to prioritise the well-being of the organisation and its stakeholders.[5] The US Merit Systems Protection Board provides resources to help implement the merit system principles and avoid prohibited personnel practices .

When we talk of merit-based governance, India provides a good case study. India's multiple diversity of culture, language, caste, religion, and ethnicity provides a paradox between the need for inclusivity and the need for effective governance. While the Indian electorate is generally discerning, there is empirical evidence that caste and religion often override the merit of the candidates and, thereby, effective governance. Uttar Pradesh (UP), Bihar,

1. https://www.opm.gov/policy-data-oversight/performance-management/reference-materials/more-topics/merit-system-principles-and-performance-management/

2. https://journals.sagepub.com/doi/full/10.1177/1056492619852170

3. https://www.linkedin.com/pulse/politics-leadership-navigating-intersection-joseph-diroma-ncc

4. https://www.sciencedirect.com/science/article/pii/S2210422416300843

5. https://www.mspb.gov/studies/studies/The_Merit_System_Principles_Keys_to_Managing_the_Federal_Workforce_1371890.pdf

Jharkhand, and Chhattisgarh are some of the many examples. Populist 'welfarism' or 'freebies' affect their electoral choices at the cost of merit, as we have seen in Delhi and Punjab. As a consequence, these states have not made progress proportionate to their potential, and the benefits of social justice have not reached those for whom it was meant. Thus, central governments have nominated technocrats as ministers at different times. The same thing can be seen in the present government.

The merit system principles are important because they provide delegation, accountability, empowerment, and flexibility, which are essential for a functioning federal workplace.[6] These principles are designed to ensure that federal personnel management is implemented consistently with the expectations of an efficient, effective, fair, open, and politically unbiased system staffed by honest, competent, and dedicated employees.[7] They serve as the foundation for the standards of ethical conduct applied to all federal employees, recognising that public service is a public trust and that employees are obligated to honour that trust by respecting and adhering to the constitution, laws, and ethical principles of government service.[8] The merit system principles also provide a framework for responsible behaviour and are key to mission success.[9] They play a crucial role in maintaining high standards of integrity, conduct, and concern for the public interest, which is essential for the effective functioning of government agencies.[10]

---

6. https://www.attorneymahoney.com/blog/2020/september/why-are-the-merit-system-principles-important-/

7. https://en.wikipedia.org/wiki/Merit_system

8. https://www.opm.gov/policy-data-oversight/performance-management/reference-materials/more-topics/merit-system-principles-and-performance-management/

9. https://www.mspb.gov/msp/msp4.htm

10. https://www.mspb.gov/msp/FAQ.htm

Merit-Based Politics

The idea of selecting politicians to contest elections based on merit and qualifications is an interesting concept that has been debated in political theory. While the concept of meritocracy, where individuals are chosen for roles based on their abilities and achievements, is common in various fields, applying it directly to the selection of politicians raises several practical and philosophical challenges.

This chapter attempts to focus on injecting merit and ethics into political leadership. It is distressing that, as per the article, 'From Kashmir to Kerala, many CMs, ex-CMs are under ED probe', by Deeptiman Tiwari, Indian Express, dated 1 February 2024, seventeen chief ministers and ex-chief ministers were under investigation by the Enforcement Directorate (ED) for corruption and misappropriation. Thus, there is a strong case to look at the existing practices in political discourse to make the election process and governance ethical and merit-based while retaining inclusivity and public representation.

Here are some considerations:

Qualifications and Criteria: Determining the qualifications and criteria for political leadership can be subjective. What constitutes 'merit' in politics is complex and may vary depending on the values and priorities of a society. It is challenging to establish universally agreed-upon criteria that define political merit.

Democracy and Representation: In democratic systems, there is a fundamental principle that political leaders are elected by the people. Imposing strict merit-based criteria might be seen as undemocratic, as it could limit the choices available to voters and disregard the principle of representation. This is not a convincing argument, as it places the cart before the horse. We have recommended solutions for these problems in Chapter XVI on Indian politics.

Diverse Skill Sets: Political leadership requires a diverse set of skills, including effective communication, negotiation, empathy, and an understanding of public sentiment. While educational and professional qualifications are important, they might not capture all the qualities needed for effective political leadership.

Potential for Elitism: Strict meritocratic approaches could lead to the concentration of political power among a perceived intellectual or professional elite. This might exclude individuals from diverse backgrounds who bring different perspectives and experiences.

Election Dynamics: Elections are dynamic processes influenced by various factors such as public opinion, campaign strategies, and political dynamics. Relying solely on merit-based selection might not align with the unpredictable nature of electoral politics.

Public Perception: The perception of political leaders as representatives of the people is crucial for the legitimacy of governance. If leaders are perceived as imposed based on merit alone, it could lead to a disconnect between the leaders and the public.

While the concept of meritocracy in politics has its challenges, there is ongoing discussion about how to ensure that political leaders have the necessary skills, knowledge, and integrity. Many political systems have eligibility criteria, such as age and citizenship requirements, but these are often minimal compared to the broader concept of merit.

Decoding Technocratic Models

At the heart of merit-based leadership lies the technocratic model, a system that places a premium on technical expertise and specialised knowledge. In this governance approach, leaders ascend to their positions based on a track record of professional accomplishments, technical prowess, and a demonstrated ability to navigate the complexities of their respective domains. The essence of technocratic governance is a commitment to leveraging specialised knowledge as the linchpin for addressing multifaceted societal challenges.

The benefits of technocratic governance are:

Efficiency and Expertise: One of the primary virtues attributed to technocratic governance is the promise of heightened efficiency. Leaders chosen for their technical acumen are poised to make informed and prompt decisions, drawing on their deep understanding of intricate issues within their purview.

Informed Decision-Making: The meritocratic approach ensures that decision-makers possess a nuanced understanding of complex challenges, be it in the realms of economics, healthcare, or technology. This depth of knowledge facilitates the formulation of policies that are not only well-informed but also tailored to address the intricacies of contemporary issues.

Long-Term Planning: Technocrats, by their technical backgrounds, often bring a forward-looking perspective to governance. The emphasis on long-term strategic planning distinguishes this model, with leaders focusing on sustainable solutions that extend beyond immediate concerns.

The major drawbacks of technocratic governance are explained below:

Democratic Legitimacy: However, the merits of technocratic governance come with their own set of challenges. A significant drawback is the potential erosion of democratic legitimacy. Leaders chosen for their technical prowess may lack a popular mandate, raising concerns about representation and accountability to the broader public.

Narrow Focus: While technocrats excel in their specialised domains, there's a risk of a narrow focus. Governance demands a holistic understanding of societal needs, and an overemphasis on technical expertise might inadvertently lead to overlooking broader social, cultural, and ethical dimensions.

Limited Public Participation: The merit-based system, while efficient, may sideline public participation in decision-making. The exclusion of diverse voices can result in policies that, while technically sound, lack the crucial element of social acceptance and inclusivity.

Debating the Merits and Demerits

Proponents of technocratic governance argue that, in an increasingly complex world, decisions demand specialised knowledge. They contend that a merit-based system ensures that leaders are equipped to tackle intricate challenges effectively. The efficiency and precision brought by technocrats can be crucial in navigating complex economic, scientific, and technological landscapes.

Critics, however, raise concerns about the potential detachment from democratic principles. They argue that governance is not solely a technical exercise but a social contract that requires broad representation. The risk of insularity and a lack of diversity in decision-making can lead to policies that are divorced from the lived realities of the population.

The discourse on technocratic governance underscores the importance of striking a balance. While technical expertise is invaluable, it should be complemented by a commitment to democratic values, inclusivity, and a holistic understanding of societal needs. The ideal system is one where proficiency meets responsiveness, ensuring that governance serves both the techn ical demands of the issues at hand and the broader aspirations of the people.

Recommendations

Apropos, we will stick our neck out and suggest measures that would promote merit-based political leadership without compromising on the inclusive and representative nature of democracy. The following provisions are worth consideration:

Character Audit: Politics is synonymous with crime, corruption, and poor ethics. Forty-three per cent of MPs in the Indian Parliament elected in 2019 had criminal records. The criminal record of aspiring political candidates needs to be examined. A yardstick should be laid down, and candidates not meeting those criteria should be banned from standing in elections. The suitable agency to do this would be a collegium comprising members of the judiciary (serving or retired) and the Election Commission. They should be empowered to investigate the background of doubtful individuals. This being a matter of critical importance, the principle of 'innocent till proven guilty' needs to be dispensed with in the public interest. Necessary safeguards need to be incorporated in the interest of fair play and justice.

Education Qualification: Suitable qualifications should be stipulated for MPs and MLA/MLCs (Members of the Legislative Assembly/Members of the Legislative Council). It is proposed that the minimum qualification for MPs be graduation and for MLA/MLCs be Class X, in keeping with the minimum education requirement for the lowest government jobs. In the interest of inclusivity and diversity, the elections at the district and gram panchayat level should be without education qualification for the next ten years, after which the education limit should be stipulated as Class X. Politics is a serious profession with immense responsibilities. A person aspiring to public service must educate and skill himself for the responsibility as a public representative in the same manner as an aspiring candidate prepares himself over the years for the civil services examination.

While it will always be the prerogative of the government in power to appoint various ministers, it is important to highlight that Defence Minister Manohar Parrikar, an engineer by education and collaborative in his functioning, understood the nuances and complexities of defence way better than any other minister of defence earlier or later. Presently, we have a career diplomat as the foreign minister who is navigating the complexities of foreign relations deftly in this complex geopolitical and geoeconomic environment. There was a case where one foreign minister read the wrong speech at the UN General Assembly. It would never happen with professionals. The same requirement goes for all the ministries.

Declaration of Assets: Every political aspirant should be required to declare their assets. While this is a procedural requirement today, it is not being followed honestly and is not leading to any action where the assets are found to be beyond their declared sources of income. All such candidates, whether first-timers or standing for re-election, must be rejected if their assets are beyond declared sources of income or are seen to have concealed or furnished false information. It is a direct reflection of integrity, and they will only promote corruption. Further, suitable action should be initiated against such cases.

Objective Evaluation and Accountability: All candidates must be evaluated on objective criteria of delivery and performance in the context of their promises and manifestos, and those need to be made public. Bihar is a perfect case study where, despite caste-based politics, the marginalised remain where they were half a century earlier, while their chosen representatives have amassed wealth.

Television Debates: To ensure the quality of political governance, it is strongly recommended that the candidates aspiring to be MPs, MLAs/MLCs, and ministers participate in a debate, US style. They should face a panel of learned citizens on their vision, integrity, skills, policies, and programmes and how they plan to finance and achieve them. It should be mandatory for parties to announce their chief minister and prime minister candidates before the elections.

Professional Public Service Education (PPSE): How does one define a career in politics? Can it be called a job (*naukri*)? Can it be called a social service or a hobby? Can anyone be fork-lifted from the sports field, Bollywood, etc., to be a politician?

Well, India is an extremely complex country that requires a good understanding of multiple perspectives—constitutional, legal, historical, social, cultural, religious, civilisational, technological, economic, governance, environmental, national security, human rights, international relations, ethics, etc. Thus, a suitable education curriculum (PPSE) needs to be designed as part of Political Science, which all aspiring political candidates should be mandated to attend and pass the test to be eligible for electoral politics at the state and national levels. This will prepare them for the onerous task of national governance, which, as of today, needs no qualification whatsoever.

None of the Above (NOTA) and Recall: The present system of election can be defined as 'Fire and Forget' for five years. There has to be a serious provision of NOTA in elections and 'recall' when an elected representative fails to measure up to the ethical standards and delivery during their tenure.

In the intricate dance between proficiency and leadership responsibilities, technocratic models offer a unique approach to governance. A cursory comparison of Indian politicians over the decades highlights the difference between those with professional backgrounds and those without.

The potential benefits in terms of efficiency, expertise, and long-term planning are compelling. However, the drawbacks, particularly regarding democratic legitimacy and a potential lack of inclusivity, demand careful consideration. The road ahead involves navigating this nuanced terrain, seeking a delicate balance that harnesses the merits of technical expertise while upholding the democratic ideals that form the foundation of inclusive governance. In practice, societies tend to rely on a combination of qualifications, experience, and the democratic process to select political leaders. Striking a balance between merit and democratic representation remains a complex and evolving challenge in political theory and practice. The criteria for choosing political candidates may vary depending on the specific context, political system, and level of government (local, regional, national). Selecting the right candidate is crucial for effective governance and representation. Singapore is the perfect example of what meritorious and value-based political leadership can achieve.

The measures recommended will go a long way in promoting merit-based governance without diluting the representative character of democracy.

CHAPTER 12

◆◆◆

The Internet and Digital Movements

The Internet as a New Force in Politics

In the early days of the Internet, few could have predicted how profoundly this digital tool would reshape political landscapes across the globe. What started as a platform for information sharing has evolved into a powerful mechanism for political mobilisation, enabling movements to operate independently of politicians and traditional political institutions. The rise of digital activism, open-source governance, and decentralised political movements has fundamentally altered the relationship between citizens and power.

In this chapter, we explore the transformative role of the Internet in modern politics, focusing on the birth of digital movements that challenge the authority of politicians and political elites. We examine key examples from recent history where digital platforms have become the epicentre of political action. We also delve into the concept of open-source governance, where the collective will of the people is directly expressed through online platforms, bypassing traditional political structures altogether.

The Internet has empowered citizens to redefine politics in ways previously unimaginable, creating opportunities for more direct, inclusive, and participatory governance. However, it has also presented significant challenges in terms of accountability, misinformation, and the digital divide. As we explore these issues, we will examine whether the Internet can truly facilitate a world of *politics without politicians*.

The Internet's Political Potential

A New Political Arena

Before the Internet, political power was largely concentrated in the hands of politicians, parties, and elite institutions. Political movements, particularly those challenging the status quo, had to rely on traditional media, political rallies, or grassroots organising, all of which required significant resources and connections. The Internet changed this dynamic by creating a new political arena where anyone with access to a digital device could participate.

Blogs, forums, and eventually social media platforms democratised political discourse, allowing individuals to engage in political conversations without needing to navigate the gatekeepers of traditional media. For the first time, people could bypass mainstream channels and directly communicate their political ideas to a global audience. This decentralisation of political dialogue marked the beginning of the Internet's transformation into a tool for activism and movement-building.

The Emergence of Social Media as a Political Powerhouse

The rise of social media platforms like Facebook, Twitter, and YouTube in the mid-2000s revolutionised the way political movements operate. Social media provided a space where citizens could share information, organise protests, and challenge political authorities with unprecedented speed and scale. Political movements no longer needed to rely on politicians or traditional media to gain traction; they could mobilise large groups of people through viral content, hashtags, and online campaigns.

One of the key features of social media is its immediacy. In the past, political organising could take weeks or even months, but now, a tweet or Facebook post can reach millions of people in seconds. This real-time engagement has allowed movements to respond rapidly to political developments, making them more agile and adaptive than traditional political institutions.

Moreover, social media has created a space where marginalised voices, often excluded from mainstream political discourse, can be amplified. Through platforms like Twitter, activists from across the globe have been able to share their stories, mobilise support, and build solidarity across borders, creating a truly global political dialogue.

Case Studies: Digital Movements in Action

The Arab Spring: A Digital Revolution

The Arab Spring stands as one of the most significant examples of the Internet's ability to fuel political movements. Beginning in late 2010, a series of protests and uprisings swept through the Arab world, toppling autocratic regimes in Tunisia, Egypt, and Libya, among others. While the root causes of these uprisings were deeply political—frustration with corrupt, authoritarian rule, high unemployment, and economic instability—the Internet played a critical role in catalysing and sustaining the protests.

In Tunisia, the self-immolation of Mohamed Bouazizi, a street vendor protesting police corruption, sparked outrage across the country. This outrage was rapidly amplified through social media, with videos of protests and government repression spreading across Facebook and Twitter. Social media allowed protestors to coordinate demonstrations, share information about police tactics, and gain international attention.

In Egypt, platforms like Facebook and Twitter were used to organise mass protests in Tahrir Square, leading to the eventual ousting of President Hosni Mubarak. The role of social media in these uprisings was so significant that some dubbed the Arab Spring a 'Facebook Revolution'. While the outcomes of these movements varied, the Internet's role in galvanising political action was undeniable. It provided citizens with a tool to challenge entrenched political powers in ways that were previously impossible.

#MeToo: A Movement Without Borders

The #MeToo movement, which exploded onto the global stage in 2017, is another example of the Internet's power to ignite social and political movements. What began as a hashtag in response to sexual harassment allegations against Hollywood mogul Harvey Weinstein quickly became a global phenomenon, as women around the world used social media to share their own experiences of sexual harassment and abuse.

#MeToo showed how the Internet could provide a platform for collective action that transcended geographic and cultural boundaries. It empowered women to speak out in a way that traditional institutions, such as the media or the legal system, had often failed to do. The decentralised nature of the movement—where no single person or organisation was in charge—allowed it to grow organically, with people from all walks of life participating.

While MeToo was not explicitly a political movement in the traditional sense, it had profound political implications. The movement led to legislative changes, corporate policies, and the downfall of powerful figures who had previously been shielded by their status. It also sparked a global conversation about power, gender, and accountability, demonstrating how the Internet can be used to address deeply entrenched societal issues outside of the traditional political framework.

#BlackLivesMatter: The Power of Hashtags

Another key example of a digital movement is #BlackLivesMatter, which began in 2013 after the acquittal of George Zimmerman in the killing of Trayvon Martin. What started as a hashtag on Twitter quickly evolved into a global movement against police violence and systemic racism. #BlackLivesMatter, like #MeToo, was decentralised, with no single leader or organisation in charge. Instead, it relied on social media to coordinate protests, raise awareness, and build solidarity.

The Internet allowed #BlackLivesMatter to spread rapidly across the world, with protests taking place in cities from New York to London to Johannesburg. The movement also used digital tools to document police violence, often through viral videos shared on platforms like Twitter and Instagram. These videos became powerful symbols of the movement, forcing both the media and politicians to confront the realities of police brutality.

One of the most significant aspects of #BlackLivesMatter is how it challenged traditional political hierarchies. Unlike past civil rights movements, which were often led by charismatic leaders or organised through established institutions, #BlackLivesMatter was a grassroots, Internet-driven movement. It operated outside the framework of formal politics, relying on the collective power of individuals rather than politicians or parties.

Open-Source Governance: A New Model of Political Participation

The Concept of Open-Source Governance

While digital movements have reshaped political activism, the Internet has also given rise to new models of governance. One of the most intriguing is open-source governance, a system in which citizens participate directly in decision-making processes through digital platforms. This model, inspired by the open-source software movement, emphasises transparency, collaboration, and decentralised control.

In traditional political systems, decisions are made by elected representatives or government officials. Open-source governance, on the other hand, allows citizens to propose, discuss, and vote on policies in real-time. The idea is to create a more inclusive, participatory form of democracy where people are directly involved in shaping the laws and policies that govern their lives.

One of the key advantages of open-source governance is that it allows for a more dynamic and responsive political system. Rather than waiting for election cycles or lobbying politicians, citizens can engage in governance continuously, making real-time decisions based on current events. This model also encourages a more informed and engaged electorate, as people are incentivised to learn about the issues and participate in meaningful ways.

Iceland's Crowdsourced Constitution

One of the most well-known examples of open-source governance in practice is Iceland's crowdsourced constitution. In the wake of the 2008 financial crisis, which devastated the country's economy, Iceland's citizens demanded political reform. As part of this process, the government initiated a project to rewrite the country's constitution, involving citizens in the drafting process through digital platforms.

Using social media and online forums, Icelanders were able to comment on drafts, suggest changes, and vote on key issues. The process was designed to be transparent and participatory, allowing citizens to have a direct say in shaping their country's future. While the final version of the constitution has yet to be fully implemented, the project was a groundbreaking experiment in open-source governance, demonstrating the potential for digital platforms to facilitate direct citizen participation in politics.

Liquid Democracy: Blurring the Lines Between Representation and Direct Participation

Another example of open-source governance is the concept of 'liquid democracy', a political system that blends elements of direct and representative democracy. In a liquid democracy, citizens can either vote directly on policy issues or delegate their vote to a trusted individual who they believe is better informed on the issue. This system allows for more flexibility and customisation in political participation, as citizens can choose how involved they want to be on any given issue.

Liquid democracy has been implemented on a small scale by political organisations like the German Pirate Party, which used digital platforms to allow members to vote on party policies in real-time. While liquid democracy is still in its experimental phase, it represents a significant shift in how we think about governance in the digital age. By giving citizens more control over the decision-making process, liquid democracy challenges the traditional role of politicians as intermediaries between the people and power.

The Shift in Political Power Dynamics

The Decline of Political Gatekeepers

The rise of digital movements and open-source governance has led to a profound shift in political power dynamics. Traditionally, politicians, political parties, and government institutions have acted as gatekeepers, controlling access to political power and decision-making. However, the Internet has disrupted this system, allowing citizens to bypass these gatekeepers and engage in politics directly.

One of the key ways this shift has manifested is in the decline of traditional political institutions. Voter turnout has been declining in many democracies as citizens increasingly turn to digital platforms to express their political views. Political parties, once the primary vehicles for political engagement, have struggled to adapt to this new reality. Many people, particularly younger generations, are more likely to engage with politics through social media or grassroots movements than through formal party structures.

The Rise of Digital Leaders

As traditional political leaders and institutions have struggled to maintain their relevance, new types of political leaders have emerged in the digital space. These digital leaders are often activists, influencers, or even anonymous individuals who use platforms like Twitter, Instagram, or TikTok to build followings and mobilise political action. Unlike traditional politicians, digital leaders do not need to be elected or hold formal office to exert influence.

One of the most notable examples of a digital leader is Greta Thunberg, the Swedish climate activist who gained global attention through her school strike for climate action. Thunberg used social media to spread her message, and her digital presence helped spark a global youth movement for climate action. Despite not holding any formal political position, Thunberg has become one of the most influential voices on climate policy, showing how digital leaders can shape political discourse without relying on traditional political institutions.

The Challenges of Digital Politics

Misinformation and the Dark Side of Digital Movements

While the Internet has empowered political movements and opened up new forms of governance, it has also created significant challenges. One of the most pressing issues is the spread of misinformation and disinformation online. Digital platforms, particularly social media, are often used to spread false or misleading information, which can undermine political movements or skew public opinion.

Misinformation campaigns, often driven by political actors or foreign governments, have been used to manipulate elections, sow division, and undermine trust in democratic institutions. The 2016 US presidential election and the Brexit referendum are two high-profile examples of how digital platforms have been used to spread misinformation on a massive scale.

The Digital Divide: Inequality in Access and Participation

Another challenge of digital politics is the digital divide—the gap between those who have access to the Internet and those who do not. While the Internet has the potential to democratise political participation, not everyone has equal access to digital tools. In many parts of the world, Internet access is still limited or non-existent, particularly in rural areas or among lower-income populations.

Even in countries with widespread Internet access, digital literacy varies significantly. Many people lack the skills to navigate online platforms effectively or to critically evaluate the information they encounter. This can lead to unequal participation in digital movements and open-source governance, as only those with access to and knowledge of digital tools can fully engage in these new political spaces.

The Future of Politics Without Politicians

How Will Politicians Adapt?

As digital movements and open-source governance continue to grow in influence, traditional politicians and political institutions will need to adapt. Some politicians have already embraced digital tools, using social media to connect with constituents or incorporating online platforms into their campaigns. However, many politicians remain wary of the Internet's disruptive potential, particularly as digital movements often operate outside of formal political channels.

The future of politics will likely involve a hybrid model, where traditional political institutions work alongside digital movements to address the needs of citizens. Politicians who can effectively leverage digital tools and engage with online communities will be better positioned to remain relevant in this new political landscape.

The Role of Technology in Shaping Future Democracies

Looking forward, technology will continue to play a critical role in shaping the future of democracy. Innovations such as blockchain, AI, and decentralised platforms have the potential to further democratise political participation and governance. For example, blockchain technology could be used to create secure, transparent voting systems, while AI could help governments analyse public opinion and make more informed policy decisions.

However, the success of these technologies will depend on addressing the challenges of misinformation, digital inequality, and accountability. As digital movements and open-source governance continue to evolve, it will be crucial to ensure that they remain inclusive, transparent, and responsive to the needs of all citizens, not just those with the loudest voices or the most resources.

The Internet has transformed politics in ways that were unimaginable just a few decades ago. From the Arab Spring to #BlackLivesMatter, digital movements have shown that political power no longer resides solely in the hands of politicians or political parties. Instead, it is increasingly dispersed among ordinary citizens who use the Internet to organise, mobilise, and demand change.

Open-source governance and liquid democracy represent new models of political participation that challenge the traditional role of politicians as intermediaries between the people and power. While these digital innovations offer exciting possibilities for more direct, participatory governance, they also raise significant challenges, particularly in terms of misinformation, inequality, and accountability.

As we move further into the digital age, the question of whether we can have *politics without politicians* remains an open one. What is clear, however, is that the Internet has forever changed the way we engage with politics, shifting power from elites to the people and opening up new possibilities for how we govern ourselves in the twenty-first century.

The latest technology toolkit is AI that instills both hopes and anxiety in how it is going to change the world, and politics will not be left untouched.

PART V

The Future of Politics Without Politicians

CHAPTER 13

◆◆◆

The Role of Civil Society in Governance: How NGOs, Think Tanks, and Grassroots Movements Shape Policy

Civil society has evolved into one of the most significant forces in modern governance, stepping into roles traditionally held by politicians and state institutions. With growing disillusionment toward political elites and formal governance structures, civil society organisations (CSOs) like non-governmental organisations (NGOs), think tanks, and grassroots movements have emerged as critical actors in shaping policy, advocating for rights, and holding governments accountable.

Civil society, in its broadest definition, refers to the collective of organisations and institutions that exist between the government, the private sector, and individual citizens. This realm of independent groups, which includes NGOs, think tanks, community organisations, and advocacy groups, serves to represent the interests and needs of society, often focusing on marginalised or underrepresented communities. Civil society operates outside formal political systems, allowing it to pursue long-term goals, hold governments accountable, and directly engage with citizens in ways that transcend electoral cycles and party politics.

This chapter explores how civil society is reshaping governance. We begin by defining civil society and its role in modern governance before diving into specific case studies to illustrate how NGOs, think tanks, and grassroots movements have stepped into political roles to bridge gaps in governance.

What Is Civil Society?

Civil society encompasses a wide array of organisations and institutions that function independently of the government, family, and business sectors. These groups advocate for social, political, and economic reforms, often pushing for transparency, accountability, and policies that address issues of public welfare. Examples of civil society actors include:

Non-Governmental Organisations: These are independent organisations that focus on social, humanitarian, or environmental goals, often providing services in areas where governments fail to act.

Think Tanks: Research institutions that conduct policy analysis and offer recommendations to governments and international bodies. Think tanks bridge the gap between academia and government, ensuring that research is applied to real-world policy-making.

Grassroots Movements: These are citizen-led movements that advocate for political or social change, often emerging in response to specific issues like economic inequality, climate justice, or human rights.

NGOs as Political Actors: Bridging Gaps in Governance

In many parts of the world, NGOs have taken on political roles traditionally held by governments, especially in areas where state institutions are weak or corrupt. By providing critical services, advocating for marginalised groups, and influencing public policy, NGOs have emerged as essential political actors. They often operate independently of government influence, allowing them to focus on long-term, humanitarian, or social justice objectives.

The Growing Influence of NGOs

NGOs have evolved from advocacy groups to major players in global governance, stepping in where governments are either unwilling or unable to act. In fragile states or conflict zones, NGOs often provide services such as healthcare, education, disaster relief, and humanitarian aid. Their flexibility and independence enable them to respond quickly to crises, something government institutions may struggle to do.

Moreover, NGOs engage in advocacy work, pushing for policy reforms at local, national, and international levels. Organisations like Amnesty International and Human Rights Watch hold governments accountable for human rights abuses, while environmental NGOs like Greenpeace advocate for policies that address climate change.

Case Study 1: Doctors Without Borders (Médecins Sans Frontières)

Founded in 1971, Doctors Without Borders (MSF) is one of the most prominent examples of an NGO that has assumed a political role in governance. Operating in conflict zones and areas affected by natural disasters, MSF provides healthcare in regions where governments have collapsed or are incapable of delivering essential services.

MSF's work highlights the political implications of humanitarian aid. In Syria, for example, MSF operates in rebel-controlled areas, providing medical care to civilians and combatants. By doing so, MSF challenges the authority of the state and highlights the deficiencies of the existing political system. MSF also advocates for international intervention when governments or armed groups impede humanitarian efforts, demonstrating how NGOs can act as political actors by stepping into roles traditionally reserved for politicians and state institutions.

Case Study 2: Amnesty International

Amnesty International, founded in 1961, exemplifies how NGOs can shape governance through human rights advocacy. Amnesty does not align with political parties, yet its work has profound political consequences. By conducting research on human rights abuses and pressuring governments to uphold international human rights standards, Amnesty has become a powerful force in global governance.

Amnesty's campaigns, such as those against the death penalty and torture, have led to significant policy changes worldwide. The organisation's public campaigns mobilise citizens to advocate for the release of political prisoners and the protection of fundamental freedoms, showcasing the power of NGOs to shape political discourse and influence policy from outside the formal political system.

Challenges for NGOs as Political Actors

While NGOs have emerged as important players in governance, they face several challenges. Critics argue that NGOs may undermine local governments by providing services that should be the responsibility of the state, creating a dependency on foreign aid. Additionally, NGOs are sometimes accused of lacking accountability since their funding often comes from private donors or foreign governments, raising questions about whom they truly serve.

Think Tanks and Policy-Making: The Brains Behind Governance

Think tanks play a crucial role in shaping public policy by conducting research and offering evidence-based recommendations to governments. Unlike politicians, who are constrained by electoral cycles and party interests, think tanks can take a long-term view and focus on the strategic challenges that governments face.

The Role of Think Tanks in Governance

Think tanks bridge the gap between academic research and government decision-making. They produce policy recommendations on issues ranging from economics and national security to social policy and international relations. By providing specialised knowledge, think tanks ensure that government policies are informed by the latest research and evidence.

Think tanks also play a key role in influencing public opinion and shaping policy debates. Through publications, media appearances, and conferences, they advocate for specific policy solutions and push issues to the top of the political agenda. Many think tanks are closely connected to government officials, political parties, and business leaders, which allows them to insert their ideas directly into the policy-making process.

Case Study 1: The Brookings Institution

Founded in 1916, the Brookings Institution is one of the most influential think tanks in the US Brookings researches a wide range of issues, from economic policy to international relations, and its work has shaped US Government policy for over a century. During the Great Depression, Brookings played a critical role in advising President Franklin D. Roosevelt's administration on economic recovery strategies.

Brookings' interdisciplinary research model allows it to provide comprehensive policy solutions, making it a key player in shaping the US domestic and foreign policy agenda. Brookings scholars are regularly invited to testify before Congress, and their recommendations have influenced policies on healthcare reform, climate change, and national security.

Case Study 2: The RAND Corporation

Founded in 1948, the RAND Corporation is known for its

quantitative research methods and its work on national security. RAND's research has shaped US defence policy, particularly during the Cold War, when it advised the government on strategies for nuclear deterrence and arms control.

RAND's influence extends beyond defence, with significant contributions to healthcare policy, including research that informed the development of the Affordable Care Act. RAND's evidence-based approach to policy-making has made it a trusted adviser for governments worldwide.

Challenges Facing Think Tanks

Despite their influence, think tanks face challenges related to independence and funding. Many think tanks rely on donations from corporations, governments, or private foundations, raising concerns about potential conflicts of interest. To maintain credibility, think tanks must ensure transparency in their funding sources and guard against donor influence.

In addition, think tanks face increasing competition for attention in the digital age, where information is abundant and easily accessible. To remain relevant, think tanks must adapt to the changing media landscape by engaging with digital platforms and communicating their findings in accessible ways.

Grassroots Movements and Citizen-Led Governance

Grassroots movements are often citizen-led efforts that emerge in response to specific social, political, or economic issues. Unlike formal political organisations, grassroots movements are typically decentralised and rely on collective action to advocate for change. These movements have become powerful forces in governance, particularly in advocating for marginalised or underrepresented communities.

The Power of Grassroots Movements

Grassroots movements are characterised by their bottom-up approach to governance. These movements often emerge when citizens feel that traditional political institutions are not addressing their concerns. By mobilising large groups of people, grassroots movements can exert significant pressure on governments and push for reforms.

One of the strengths of grassroots movements is their inclusivity. Because they are decentralised, grassroots movements provide a platform for people from all walks of life to participate in governance. This inclusivity allows movements to build broad coalitions and create a sense of ownership among participants.

Case Study 1: The Occupy Movement

The Occupy Movement, which began in 2011 in the US, is a prominent example of a grassroots movement that challenged traditional governance structures. The movement, which protested economic inequality and corporate influence in politics, operated without formal leadership and relied on collective decision-making. Occupy's slogan, 'We are the 99%', highlighted the movement's focus on economic justice and its critique of the political elite.

While the Occupy Movement eventually lost momentum, it succeeded in bringing issues of economic inequality and corporate power to the forefront of public discourse. The movement's decentralised, participatory model of governance allowed citizens to express their frustrations with the political system and demand accountability from political leaders.

Challenges Facing Grassroots Movements

While grassroots movements have the potential to effect significant change, they also face challenges. Without formal leadership structures, movements may struggle to achieve long-term goals or respond to changing political environments. Additionally, grassroots movements often rely on digital platforms for communication and organisation, making them vulnerable to government surveillance or online disinformation campaigns.

The Future of Civil Society in Governance

As civil society continues to expand its role in governance, its relationship with traditional political institutions will likely evolve. Civil society organisations often complement government efforts by providing expertise, advocating for reforms, and holding governments accountable. Civil society organisations may take on more direct governance roles in fragile or failed states, providing essential services and advocating for policy changes.

The future of civil society in governance will also depend on its ability to navigate challenges related to accountability, access, and government opposition. Governments, particularly in authoritarian regimes, may view civil society as a threat and impose restrictions on its activities. Civil society organisations must also ensure that they are transparent and accountable to the communities they serve, particularly when their funding comes from foreign donors or private foundations. Civil society has become an indispensable force in modern governance, stepping into roles traditionally held by politicians and state institutions. NGOs, think tanks, and grassroots movements have shown that governance is not the exclusive domain of elected officials; rather, it is a collective responsibility that involves all sectors of society.

Through advocacy, research, and direct action, civil society organisations have shaped policies, provided critical services, and held governments accountable. As the world faces increasingly complex challenges, from climate change to human rights abuses, civil society will continue to play a key role in shaping the future of governance, ensuring that it is more inclusive, participatory, and responsive to the needs of all people.

CHAPTER 14

◆◆◆

Politics Sans Politicians: Practical Obstacles in a Transition to a System Without Political Elites

In an age of growing scepticism toward political elites, the idea of eliminating politicians and embracing more direct forms of governance has gained traction in some circles. Citizens around the world, frustrated by political corruption, gridlock, and lack of representation, are increasingly drawn to alternative models such as open-source governance, decentralised decision-making, or even systems that rely more heavily on technology and civic engagement rather than elected officials.

Yet, while the allure of *politics without politicians* is strong, there are several practical obstacles to such a transition. Trust in political processes, the complexities of systemic transitions, and ensuring democratic accountability are all major hurdles that cannot be ignored. This chapter delves into these challenges, outlining the significant barriers to eliminating politicians from governance and why reforming political institutions may be more feasible than removing them entirely.

The Role of Public Trust in Political Systems

One of the most fundamental challenges in removing politicians from governance is the issue of public trust. For centuries, political systems have relied on elected officials to serve as intermediaries between the people and the state. Politicians, whether they operate in a democratic, authoritarian, or hybrid system, are traditionally seen as the legitimate representatives of the people's interests. Even though trust in politicians has eroded in many parts of the world, the concept of representative democracy remains deeply ingrained.

Erosion of Trust and Demand for Alternatives

Over the past few decades, public trust in politicians has indeed declined dramatically. Scandals involving corruption, self-interest, and lack of accountability have fuelled a growing sense of disenfranchisement among voters. From the 2008 financial crisis to various political crises in countries like Brazil, the US, and Italy, politicians have been increasingly seen as part of the problem rather than the solution.

Movements advocating for direct democracy or open-source governance have emerged in response to this crisis of trust. Proponents argue that technological advancements make it easier than ever for citizens to directly participate in governance, circumventing the need for politicians. Blockchain-based voting systems, liquid democracy models, and decentralised platforms are some of the tools being considered to enable more participatory forms of governance.

The Paradox of Public Trust

However, while distrust in politicians is widespread, the absence of any trusted alternative to traditional political institutions poses a significant problem. Paradoxically, even as citizens express dissatisfaction with their leaders, they often remain wary of new, untested systems that aim to eliminate the role of politicians altogether.

The question of legitimacy looms large: how can a new system establish itself as a trustworthy alternative to the existing order? Historically, political transitions—whether toward democracy, authoritarianism, or technocracy—have been fraught with uncertainty and risk. The absence of established political actors may lead to fears of instability or, worse, an erosion of democratic safeguards.

In this context, the removal of politicians may not necessarily restore trust in governance. Instead, it risks further undermining confidence in the system if the alternatives are perceived as unstable or easily manipulated. For any attempt to transition away from politicians, earning and maintaining public trust remains an essential challenge.

Transitioning Systems: Complexity and Institutional Inertia

Removing politicians from governance requires more than just a philosophical shift; it involves a fundamental overhaul of the institutions that form the backbone of political systems. Governments are not just composed of politicians; they are vast, bureaucratic structures that include civil servants, regulatory bodies, judicial systems, and military institutions, all of which interact in intricate ways. Transitioning away from a political system reliant on politicians would involve a reconfiguration of these institutions at every level.

The Weight of Institutional Inertia

One of the biggest challenges in transitioning to a system without politicians is institutional inertia. Governments and political systems tend to resist change due to their sheer size and complexity. Even incremental reforms within existing systems often face significant resistance as entrenched interests—whether political parties, businesses, or lobby groups—strive to maintain their influence.

Completely eliminating politicians would not only disrupt these interests but also necessitate a restructuring of how laws are made, policies are implemented, and justice is administered. This process would be complicated, time-consuming, and prone to failure if not executed with precision.

For example, how would the legislature function in the absence of elected representatives? Who would draft laws, and how would decisions be made about which policies to prioritise? The move toward direct citizen participation, while appealing in theory, raises practical questions about logistics. Coordinating decision-making processes for millions of people across various regions would require not just technological infrastructure but also new methods of consensus-building and conflict resolution.

Examples of Transition Failures

Historically, attempts to radically restructure political systems without careful planning have led to instability and unintended consequences. For example, the collapse of the Soviet Union in the early 1990s left many of its former republics struggling to establish stable political systems. In the absence of strong institutions, several of these countries experienced political and economic chaos, with power vacuums leading to corruption, authoritarianism, or civil conflict.

In more recent times, the Arab Spring revolutions of 2011 saw mass uprisings in countries like Egypt, Libya, and Tunisia, where citizens sought to overthrow corrupt, entrenched regimes. While the initial revolutions were successful in removing long-standing leaders, the transition to new systems of governance has been tumultuous. In Egypt, for example, the power vacuum left by the removal of President Hosni Mubarak in 2011 eventually led to a military coup and the re-establishment of authoritarian rule under President Abdel Fattah el-Sisi.

These examples demonstrate that while citizens may clamour for change, the complexity of transitioning from one system to another can lead to chaos if not managed carefully. The removal of politicians may create a governance vacuum, which could be exploited by opportunistic forces or result in instability.

Ensuring Democratic Accountability Without Politicians

One of the most critical roles that politicians play in representative democracies is ensuring accountability. Elected officials, in theory, are held accountable by the voters who put them into office. If they fail to deliver on their promises or act against the public interest, they risk being voted out in the next election cycle. While the system is far from perfect, it offers a mechanism for holding leaders accountable.

The Role of Elections in Accountability

Elections serve as a key mechanism for democratic accountability. Citizens choose their representatives, and those representatives are expected to govern on their behalf. Politicians, while not always trustworthy, are subject to scrutiny by the media, watchdog organisations, and, ultimately, the electorate. Regular elections provide the public with the opportunity to remove politicians who are ineffective, corrupt, or out of touch with their constituents.

In a system without politicians, how would accountability be maintained? The idea of direct democracy, where citizens vote on laws and policies themselves, raises concerns about how to ensure that decisions are made in the public interest. In traditional democracies, politicians, at least in theory, are expected to balance competing interests and make decisions that serve the broader public good. Without elected representatives to perform this function, the risk of decision-making being dominated by vocal interest groups, corporations, or wealthy individuals increases.

Risks of Technocratic or Algorithmic Governance

Some proponents of eliminating politicians argue that technology, particularly AI and algorithmic governance, could offer a solution to the problem of accountability. However, this raises its own set of concerns. If algorithms were used to make decisions, who would design them, and how would their decisions be subject to oversight?

Algorithms are not neutral; they are created by humans, and the values, biases, and assumptions of their designers can influence the outcomes. In a system where algorithms replace politicians, ensuring transparency and accountability becomes even more challenging. Moreover, algorithmic systems could be vulnerable to manipulation or hacking, potentially leading to abuses of power.

Technocratic systems, where decision-making is left to experts rather than elected officials, also pose accountability challenges. While technocrats may have specialised knowledge, they are not necessarily representative of the population at large. Decisions made by experts might prioritise efficiency or technical solutions at the expense of democratic values like equity, inclusion, or human rights.

The Risk of Authoritarianism and Power Consolidation

Another significant risk in eliminating politicians is the potential for authoritarianism or power consolidation. When politicians are removed from the equation, the vacuum left behind could be filled by unelected leaders, military figures, or technocratic elites who are not accountable to the public.

In situations where power becomes concentrated in the hands of a small group of individuals—whether technocrats, corporate executives, or military leaders—democratic principles can quickly erode. The absence of checks and balances provided by an elected legislature or judiciary increases the risk of authoritarian governance.

Historical Precedents

History is filled with examples of political systems where the removal of democratic processes led to authoritarianism. One of the clearest examples is the rise of fascist regimes in Europe in the twentieth century. In Italy, for instance, the dismantling of democratic institutions under Benito Mussolini led to the establishment of a dictatorship. Similarly, in Germany, the Weimar Republic's failure to manage political and economic crises paved the way for Adolf Hitler's rise to power and the consolidation of authoritarian rule.

In more recent times, countries like Venezuela have seen the erosion of democratic norms under leaders like Hugo Chávez and Nicolás Maduro. What began as a populist movement to challenge corrupt political elites eventually devolved into a regime marked by autocratic rule, political repression, and economic collapse.

In 2024, Bangladesh has emerged as an example of serious disruption when an established political order, a democracy, is uprooted without due diligence. The religious fundamentalist forces have exploited the vacuum and are filling up that space. Recovering the lost democratic space will be an exercise with unknown consequences that could destabilise the country. However, here we are talking of a measured, well-deliberated concept of organised public participation under the existing governance.

While the idea of eliminating politicians might appeal to those disillusioned with the current political system, the practical obstacles to such a transition are significant. Public trust, systemic complexity, accountability, and the risk of authoritarianism all pose major challenges to removing politicians from governance. Instead of seeking to eliminate politicians entirely, a more pragmatic approach may be to reform existing political institutions, making them more transparent, accountable, and responsive to the needs of citizens.

By focusing on reforms such as increasing citizen participation, improving the integrity of elections and the quality of political candidates, strengthening checks and balances, and ensuring regular accountability, societies can address the root causes of political dissatisfaction while preserving the democratic principles that ensure stability and accountability.

PART VI

◆◆◆

Stop Press

CHAPTER 15

◆◆◆

The Second Coming of Donald Trump: A Domino Moment for Global Democracy

Democracy is often hailed as the most effective form of governance. However, it manifests in various forms across the globe, shaped by each nation's unique historical, cultural, and political landscape. From the US and the UK to India, Singapore, Russia, Iran, and Turkey, democratic systems differ significantly. Pakistan stands out as an exceptional case, where a government is elected and operates under heavy influence, if not outright control, of the military, challenging conventional definitions of democracy.

In this edition of 'Stop Press', we explore recent developments in the world's oldest democracy through the lens of the book.

Trump 2.0 – The Return of Donald Trump

In a political shockwave echoing his 2016 victory, Donald J. Trump stormed back into the White House, sworn in for a second term by January 2025. For his loyal base, his return marked a triumph of resilience against the political establishment. For his critics, it was a democratic regression—an ominous re-opening of old wounds.

Trump's second presidency is more than a sequel; it is a live case study of how personalised populism, technocratic bypasses, and institutional erosion can reshape the character of democracy itself. In the context of *politics without politicians*, his governance style underscores a core tension: when power is monopolised by charismatic leaders rather than distributed through democratic institutions, personal ambition can eclipse public interest. The global consequences of Trump's return will not stop at US borders.

The 2024 Election: A Deeply Divided Mandate

The 2024 election played out against a backdrop of historic polarisation. Despite trailing in national polls, Trump eked out an Electoral College win by narrow margins across battleground states. Though he once again lost the popular vote, his victory narrative claimed a sweeping mandate against 'globalist elites' and 'woke tyranny'.

Much like 2016, Trump positioned himself as the outsider warrior. But this time, he returned with a vendetta against institutions he believes hindered his first term—the FBI (Federal Bureau of Investigation), the Department of Justice, and the press. His campaign didn't just revive grievances; it weaponised them. In doing so, Trump highlighted the central dilemma of modern democracy: charismatic leaders can leverage popular discontent to gain power without healing divisions or strengthening institutions.

Building the Court of Trump

Trump wasted no time appointing loyalists to key positions. Cabinet posts were handed to former advisers and right-wing media figures, forming a court-like circle where loyalty outweighed competence. This consolidation of personal power turned the government into an echo chamber.

Within days, Trump unleashed executive orders undoing Biden-era policies on climate, immigration, and health. Some reversals appeared less policy-driven and more personal, targeting agencies and legal frameworks that had previously challenged him. This blurring of state interests and personal retribution reveals a democracy vulnerable to personalisation.

Populism Reloaded: Rallying, Rhetoric, and Retaliation

Victory rallies resumed almost immediately. Framed as grassroots celebrations, these events often devolved into stage-managed spectacles of identity-based grievance. In them, Trump painted himself as the lone sentinel against a corrupt elite conspiracy. His movement fed off nostalgia, fear, and a disdain for nuance.

Democratic erosion, scholars warn, now unfolds through gradual undermining rather than coups. Trump's strategy, from attacking watchdog institutions to publicly discrediting court decisions, exemplifies this pattern. His narrative delegitimises all opposition, branding critics as traitors to the people.

A Foreign Policy of Instincts Over Institutions

Trump's 2025 foreign policy doctrine has made global headlines, not just for its abrupt shifts but for the upheaval it has caused. The sudden reversals have strained long-standing alliances and disrupted established international norms.

Ukraine: Trump froze arms shipments, conditioning aid on Europe paying its 'fair share'. Eastern European allies were left questioning the US commitment to their sovereignty. In a sudden and stark departure, the US abandoned Ukraine after three years of unwavering support built on the promise of 'as long as it takes'. The demand for repayment through a rare earth metals deal came as a shocking twist—an unexpected curveball in an already fragile alliance.

Russia: Secret backchannel talks with Moscow hinted at potential sanction relief, evoking fears of personal diplomacy overriding strategic consistency. Suddenly, the most ardent adversary of Russia had turned into an ally.

Iran: The Joint Comprehensive Plan of Action (JCPOA) or the Iran Nuclear Deal was scrapped by Trump during his first term. Sanctions intensified, and regional tensions escalated. As we go to print, the US-Iran direct talks under the US unilateral approach seemed to make a headway for the present under Trump 2.0. Well, it ended with a US strike on an Iranian nuclear facility in collusion with Israel, a country believed to have nuclear weapons itself. We've got to wait and watch.

Yemen: Under Joe Biden, the US had scaled down support for the Saudi-led intervention in Yemen. Trump swiftly reversed course, resuming certain arms sales. He engaged in an intense direct aerial war with Yemen, putting pressure on Iran and prioritising realpolitik over humanitarian concerns. An individual leader's quick decisions can overshadow multi-stakeholder diplomatic processes essential to sustaining peace and democratic governance.

China: Tariffs returned with vengeance as arms sales to Taiwan surged. Trump's unilateral approach amplified Beijing-Washington tensions that threaten the world economic order. The risk of confrontation rises when a single politician's combative instincts shape national policy, particularly when the administration's team is selected more for loyalty than nuanced expertise.

Canada and Mexico: Trump threatened the United States-Mexico-Canada Agreement (USMCA) renegotiations, claiming unfair trade deals. Trump's tariff war and his desire to assimilate Canada as the fifty-first state of the US turned a trusted ally and neighbour into an adversary. His desire to take over Greenland shocked the world.

North Atlantic Treaty Organization (NATO): The US is fully justified in demanding higher defence spending by NATO members. But it severely strained transatlantic unity, revealing Trump's distrust of multilateralism. It forced a review of EU security policies, including nuclear policies.

In each case, traditional diplomacy gave way to personalised, transactional leadership, a hallmark of politics ruled by individual impulse over institutional process.

Domestic Fallout: Institutions in the Crosshairs

Trump's style has been norm-breaking since day one. But in 2025, with fewer constraints, he has gone further:

- *Executive dominance* has accelerated. Bypassing Congress, Trump governs by decree and through executive orders.
- *Media antagonism* is institutionalised. Dissenting outlets are accused of sedition.
- *Judicial delegitimisation* is routine. Any court ruling against the administration is painted as partisan sabotage.

The politicisation of bureaucracy has deepened. Departments once rooted in policy are now judged by ideological conformity. The civil service shrinks under loyalty tests, and scientific agencies are sidelined.

Personality Over Policy

Trumpism is not a doctrine but a performance. Supporters cheer his bravado, not legislative milestones. Public discourse becomes about image, not ideas.

This personalist model redefines democracy. Politics becomes a contest of personalities. Laws are malleable. Institutions serve the person in office rather than the constitution. It is the government as theatre, where accountability is elusive and narrative trumps truth.

The Institutional Fallout: Ten Dominoes Tipping Over

Algorithmic Democracy: When Voters Are Data, Not Citizens

The 2024 Trump campaign wasn't just a political machine; it was a data-driven juggernaut. Gone were the town halls and grassroots engagements of old. In their place, micro-targeted ads, AI-generated content, and algorithmically optimised outreach. Trump's digital war room operated like a hedge fund calculating voter moods in real-time, then deploying precision-crafted messages to nudge behaviour. Deepfakes replaced campaign promises. Predictive analytics gauged emotional resonance. It was less about policy than it was about profiling.

But this wasn't innovation—it was manipulation. By converting voters into algorithmic subjects, Trump's campaign effectively gamified democracy. The result? A political process more akin to personalised marketing than civic dialogue. When the electorate is fed a diet of confirmation bias, dissenting views vanish into the abyss of the algorithm. The public square becomes a private loop.

This was the death knell of deliberative democracy. It marked the rise of what *politics without politicians* warns us about—a system where technological gatekeepers shape voter perception more than parties or policies. In this brave new world, elections aren't won—they're engineered. And that sets a precedent with global echoes.

Weakening of Representative Politics: The Party Is Over, The Brand Remains

In 2024, Donald Trump didn't so much lead the Republican Party as eclipse it. Gone were the days of platforms and policy caucuses; what remained was personality cult politics. Trump ran not as a Republican but as a singular force—an icon of grievance and revenge. The Grand Old Party (GOP) apparatus merely followed suit, shedding its ideological skin for a red cap and a truth-social repost.

Traditional representative politics depends on institutions and parties that mediate between citizens and the state. But Trump's direct-to-voter model rendered these obsolete. Through social media blasts and live-streamed rally tirades, he built a feedback loop where loyalty replaced debate, and slogans supplanted policy.

The implications are stark. When parties become mere amplifiers of one man's voice, they cease to be institutions of accountability. Congress becomes performative. Legislators act more like social media influencers than lawmakers. Dissent within the party isn't tolerated; it's cancelled.

The system that emerges is one of *politics without politicians,* diagnosed with urgency: a hollowed political field where representation bends to charisma and where voters choose not policies but personas. Globally, this signals a shift from democracy to demotainment, where electability depends on virality, not vision.

Technocracy Replacing Governance: The Rule of Experts, Not the People

Within days of retaking office, President Trump signed a flurry of executive orders, not to expand democratic engagement but to sidestep it. Climate protection, asylum frameworks, and healthcare mandates were overturned at the stroke of a pen. But the real pivot was subtler and more profound.

By appointing Elon Musk to head the Department of Government Efficiency (DOGE), Trump effectively outsourced governance to corporate technocrats. Bureaucracy was rebranded as a startup. The policy was filtered through innovation metrics. The catch? Musk, a private titan with sprawling interests in AI, defence, and infrastructure, now sat at the helm of public efficiency without ever facing a vote.

Technocracy may promise precision, but it often lacks legitimacy. When unelected billionaires direct policy, democracy is reduced to a boardroom, with citizens as stakeholders, not participants. Trump's government didn't eliminate red tape; it cut out the middleman of accountability.

As *politics without politicians* outlines, when power bypasses parliaments and flows to CEOs, governance becomes transactional. It's a system designed for output, not outreach. And if replicated worldwide, it could birth a new kind of governance: one where data, capital, and access matter more than ballots.

Judicial and Institutional Overreach: The Gavel in a Vice

In any healthy democracy, the judiciary serves as a neutral arbiter—a bulwark against executive overreach. But Trump's second term began with a calculated campaign to reshape that balance. From disparaging federal judges to appointing loyalists across the bench, the administration signalled a clear message: justice must align with the president's vision—or face his wrath.

The pattern is familiar and chilling. Investigations into Trump's previous tenure were labelled 'witch hunts'. Prosecutors who pressed too hard found themselves reassigned or publicly attacked. Executive actions limited oversight over agencies like the FBI and the Department of Justice (DOJ), turning watchdogs into lapdogs.

Even more concerning was the normalisation of institutional delegitimisation. Every court ruling not in Trump's favour was branded biased. Every independent agency became suspect. This erosion of public trust in neutral institutions creates a vacuum, and autocrats rush to fill it.

As *politics without politicians* cautions, the judiciary is democracy's last line of defence. Undermine it, and you open the floodgates. Across the globe, from Hungary to India, leaders have taken note. The American model of slow-burning institutional capture has become an exportable blueprint for democratic decay.

Corporate Capture of Democracy: When Billionaires Run the Bureaucracy

One of Trump's boldest and most controversial appointments in his second term was putting Elon Musk in charge of DOGE. Musk, the tech titan behind Tesla, SpaceX, and X (formerly Twitter), was handed the keys to a federal overhaul project that touched everything from procurement to infrastructure AI systems. His appointment sent shockwaves through Washington not because of his brilliance but because of his unchecked influence.

Critics warned of a dangerous merger: private capital fused with public control. Musk's sprawling corporate interests, many of which relied on federal contracts and subsidies, were now directly entangled with national policy. Conflict of interest became a feature, not a flaw.

This wasn't technocracy—it was corporate conquest of the state.

What *politics without politicians* underscores is that when corporate giants step into governance without public mandate, they don't just influence policy—they embody it. Public services risk being evaluated not by social benefit but by shareholder logic. Accountability gives way to quarterly performance metrics.

Across the globe, democracies are watching. From Silicon Valley to Singapore, corporate barons are eyeing a future not just as lobbyists but as unelected lawmakers in suits. Trump has merely normalised the trend.

Politics as Performance: Democracy, Rebranded as Entertainment

Trump's 2024 campaign played out less like an election and more like a Netflix season finale. TikTok dances replaced policy pamphlets. Influencers outpaced political analysts in shaping narratives. Campaign rallies felt like rock concerts, with chants choreographed and lighting calibrated for viral moments. Substance was sacrificed at the altar of spectacle.

With millions of followers and a direct pipeline to the base, Trump became not just a candidate but a lifestyle brand. His policies were delivered in memes, not white papers. His critiques came as stand-up bits, not structured arguments. In this environment, serious policy discussion was drowned in the algorithmic churn of attention economics.

What *politics without politicians* identifies here is a global mutation: politics becomes entertainment, and politicians become performers. In such a world, electoral success hinges less on competence and more on charisma. Institutions lose their role as arbiters of governance. Instead, audiences cheer for characters, not custodians of the republic.

The danger? When politics is scripted like reality TV, reality is scripted like politics. And governance becomes a performance where the audience claps, but no one governs.

Erosion of Civic Participation: Apathy in the Age of Hyper-Engagement

Ironically, in a hyper-connected age, democratic participation is thinning. The 2024 election saw record-breaking digital impressions but disappointing in-person turnout in several key demographics, especially young and first-time voters. Trump's digitally dominated campaign fed this paradox; millions watched, but few acted.

Why? Because civic fatigue has replaced civic duty.

Endless scandals, misinformation, and the performative nature of modern politics have numbed public engagement. Voters no longer feel empowered—they feel out-gamed. Every vote seems swallowed by the noise. Every issue is a branding exercise. When democracy feels like a product being sold, citizens stop seeing themselves as stakeholders.

Politics without politicians warns that a disengaged electorate isn't just a democratic failure; it's fertile ground for autocracy. The fewer the participants, the easier it becomes to rule unchecked. And across the world, authoritarian regimes are learning that public silence is easier to manage than public resistance.

In Trump's America, civic erosion wasn't an accident. It was collateral damage in a political war waged through saturation, cynicism, and spectacle.

Surveillance and Manipulation: Democracy's Invisible Puppet Strings

The 2024 Trump campaign elevated voter manipulation to a science. By harvesting vast troves of user data, including online behaviour, emotional triggers, and location history, campaign operatives deployed tailored messages that blurred the boundary between persuasion and psychological warfare.

AI chatbots engaged undecided voters in simulated conversations. Deepfake videos subtly recast rivals in an unfavourable light. Voter sentiment was mined, monetised, and then moulded, often without consent or awareness.

What emerged wasn't an informed electorate but a profiled, targeted, and nudged population.

As *politics without politicians* outlines, this is algorithmic autocracy in sheep's clothing. Surveillance democracies cloak their control behind code. Instead of silencing dissent with force, they redirect it with design. Instead of ballots being counted honestly, preferences are shaped before ballots are cast.

China does this openly. But in Trump's America, the tools of Silicon Valley were marshalled for democratic distortion and framed as 'smart campaigning'.

The implications are chilling. When voters are studied more than heard, democracy is no longer free—it's preprogrammed.

Hollowing of Democratic Structures: Institutions That Look Like Democracy, But Don't Act Like It

On paper, the US still had a Congress, a judiciary, and a free press. But under Trump 2.0, these pillars increasingly served symbolic functions. Congress was frequently bypassed via executive orders. The judiciary, packed with ideological loyalists, mirrored White House rhetoric. Even the press was branded 'the enemy', or fake, eroding its watchdog role.

Institutions existed, but they no longer mediated power. They echoed it.

This hollowing of governance is what *politics without politicians* calls 'democracy in drag': structures remain, but purpose evaporates. Decision-making flows vertically from one man to his inner circle, to the masses, without institutional filtration or opposition.

It's not a dictatorship, but it's not a liberal democracy either. It's the grey zone that many populist regimes now inhabit: elections without accountability, parliaments without power, courts without independence.

And it's spreading from Poland's constitutional court capture to India's erosion of civil liberties. The American example is no longer a shining light but a flickering warning.

Drift Toward Soft Authoritarianism? The Legal Authoritarian in a Red Tie

Trump didn't abolish the constitution or institutions. He didn't cancel elections. He didn't stage a coup. Yet, through legal means and populist will, he achieved a soft authoritarian drift that bent the system without breaking it.

Media critics were vilified, judges were maligned, and Congressional oversight was stonewalled. Loyalty became the price of admission to governance. All of it was done within the veneer of legality.

This is the modern strongman's method—weaponise democratic tools to subvert democratic intent.

In his second term, Trump has continued that trend, flanked by loyalists, emboldened by a divided electorate, and fuelled by a narrative that pits 'the people' against 'the system'. It's textbook illiberal democracy.

As *politics without politicians* asserts, the biggest threat to democracy today isn't the tyrant with tanks. It's the politician with a Twitter account, a loyal base, and a toolkit of legal shortcuts. The question isn't whether democracy will fall. It's whether it will slowly be drained—one executive order, one disinformation blast, one institutional surrender at a time.

Each of these, independently dangerous, together form a domino chain that threatens to irrevocably alter the architecture of democratic systems, both in America and globally.

A Global Warning and a Final Opportunity

The global democratic community is watching closely. Already, leaders from Turkey, Hungary, and the Philippines have adopted the populist template—personalise power, erode checks, and delegitimise opposition.

Trump's second term, if unchallenged by robust institutions, could mark a tipping point. But therein lies a paradox—his return may also galvanise democratic reform.

Activists, journalists, courts, and even moderate lawmakers could respond with renewed vigour. Public protests—we are already seeing some in the US, investigative journalism, and digital literacy campaigns may counteract the trend.

Democracies survive not by avoiding crisis but by responding to it. Trump's presidency might also spark the very reckoning needed to confront the vulnerabilities of politics built on personalities.

What Next?

For the argument in Politics Reimagined, the Trump presidency remains a case study in how quickly democratic norms can fray when confronted with charismatic populism and how a structural rethinking, such as direct citizen participation, stronger institutional buffers, or less centralised power, might mitigate that risk in the future.

As Trump strides into his renewed presidency, the future of American democracy stands on a knife's edge. Will institutions assert their independence or surrender to the tide of personalism? Will the electorate awaken to the cost of charismatic rule, or double down on spectacle?

For the world, the implications are immense. If the US cannot contain the authoritarian drift within a democratic framework, it sets a precedent for other nations to follow.

The lessons from this moment are clear: democracy is not just a structure of laws, but a culture of restraint, participation, and pluralism. And unless the politics of spectacle and power are held to account, the second coming of Donald Trump may well be remembered as the beginning of democracy's slow, global undoing—or its unexpected renewal. Only time will tell.

As we conclude this chapter, here is some food for thought. Democracy derives its strength from the people. Can one really complain if people approve of the leader's agenda and approach?

The strength of democracy lies in periodic elections. There will be another election in the US in four years. Who knows, these four years could be the longest four years in the history of democracy.

PART VII

◆◆◆

Conclusion

CHAPTER 16

◆◆◆

Towards a Politician-Free Future

"Those who seek power are not worthy of that power."

—Plato

Plato must have been a visionary. What he said in the fourth Century BC is true even today. For centuries, political systems around the world have been structured around the idea of elected representatives and politicians who serve as intermediaries between the government and the governed. From parliaments and congresses to local councils, these figures have long played a central role in shaping laws, policies, and governance. However, in an era marked by rapid technological change, growing political disillusionment, and the rise of decentralised digital tools, some visionaries are asking a provocative question: what if we could eliminate traditional politicians altogether?

A politician-free future envisions a political system where power no longer rests with a select group of individuals who are elected to represent the people. Instead, it imagines a system where citizens directly participate in governance, enabled by advanced technologies such as AI, blockchain, and digital platforms. This chapter systematically explores the possibilities of such a future, weighing the potential benefits, the risks, and the practical challenges of a world without traditional politicians.

The Growing Disillusionment with Politicians

The only time I trust a politician is when he calls another a liar.

—Anonymous

Before diving into the idea of a politician-free future, it's essential to understand the context that has led to the growing appetite for alternatives. In recent years, public trust in politicians has reached alarmingly low levels in many democracies. The reasons for this disillusionment are numerous and include:

Corruption: Political corruption scandals have been a persistent issue worldwide, eroding public trust in elected officials. From the Petrobras scandal in Brazil to allegations of collusion between big corporations and government officials, the perception that politicians serve special interests rather than the public good has fuelled scepticism about their role.

Gridlock and Inefficiency: In many democratic systems, political gridlock has led to a paralysis of governance. In countries like the US, partisan polarisation has made it increasingly difficult for governments to pass meaningful legislation, leaving many citizens frustrated by the lack of progress on critical issues like healthcare, climate change, and economic inequality.

Populism and Authoritarianism: The rise of populist leaders who promise to 'drain the swamp' and challenge political elites reflects a deep dissatisfaction with the status quo. However, many of these populist movements have themselves led to authoritarian tendencies, creating new problems rather than solving the old ones.

Disconnected Elites: Politicians are often viewed as part of an elite class that is disconnected from the realities faced by ordinary people. This perception is particularly strong in countries with growing income inequality, where the political class is seen as out of touch with the struggles of the average citizen.

Against this backdrop of disillusionment, many have begun to question whether the traditional role of politicians is still necessary or even desirable. Is there a way to govern more efficiently, transparently, and inclusively without relying on political elites? This question has given rise to various proposals for a future where governance is decentralised, participatory, and powered by technology rather than by individuals seeking political office.

The Tools and Technologies for a Politician-Free Future

The technological advancements of the twenty-first century have provided a fertile ground for exploring the possibility of governance without politicians. The rise of the Internet, blockchain technology, AI, and big data has opened new pathways for reimagining how societies can be governed. Here are some of the key technologies that could underpin a politician-free future:

Blockchain and Decentralised Decision-Making

Blockchain technology has been hailed as a revolutionary tool for ensuring transparency, security, and decentralisation in governance. Blockchain's distributed ledger system ensures that all transactions (or, in the case of governance, votes and decisions) are recorded transparently and cannot be altered or manipulated by any central authority.

In a politician-free future, blockchain could be used to create a decentralised system of governance where citizens vote directly on policies, laws, and budgetary decisions. This could eliminate the need for elected representatives, as decisions would be made collectively and recorded on a transparent, tamper-proof ledger.

Case Study – Decentralised Autonomous Organisations (DAOs)

DAOs are organisations that operate on blockchain technology and are governed by smart contracts rather than traditional hierarchies. DAOs allow for decision-making processes to be decentralised, with each participant having a vote proportional to their stake in the organisation. Some advocates see DAOs as a potential model for future political systems, where citizens have direct control over governance without the need for politicians.

Artificial Intelligence and Algorithmic Governance

AI could play a crucial role in a politician-free future by providing data-driven decision-making that is free from human biases and special interests. AI systems can analyse vast amounts of data, identify patterns, and recommend policy decisions based on empirical evidence rather than political ideology.

For example, AI could be used to create algorithms that allocate public resources more efficiently or predict the long-term impacts of different policy choices. These AI-driven decisions would be transparent and based on objective criteria, reducing the risk of corruption or political favouritism.

Case Study – AI in Public Services

Some cities and governments are already experimenting with AI to improve public services. In Singapore, AI is used to optimise traffic flow, while in Estonia, AI chatbots help citizens navigate government services. While these examples are still limited to administrative functions, they demonstrate the potential for AI to play a broader role in governance.

Direct Democracy Through Digital Platforms

One of the most promising aspects of a politician-free future is the possibility of direct democracy enabled by digital platforms. In a direct democracy, citizens vote on every policy issue rather than electing representatives to make decisions on their behalf. While direct democracy has been historically difficult to implement on a large scale due to logistical challenges, digital platforms make it much more feasible.

Platforms like the Swiss online voting system and Liquid Feedback (used in Germany's Pirate Party) allow citizens to vote directly on issues or delegate their votes to trusted experts in specific fields. These systems enable more direct citizen participation in governance without the need for traditional politicians.

Case Study – Switzerland's Direct Democracy

Switzerland has one of the most robust systems of direct democracy in the world, with citizens regularly voting on referendums that shape the country's laws and policies. Digital platforms could expand this model globally, allowing citizens in any country to have a direct say in their government's decisions.

Potential Benefits of a Politician-Free Future

The idea of a politician-free future is appealing to many for several reasons. The potential benefits of such a system include:

Increased Transparency and Reduced Corruption

One of the most significant advantages of a politician-free system is the potential to reduce corruption and increase transparency. By removing politicians from the equation, governance would rely more heavily on technology, algorithms, and citizen participation. Blockchain and other decentralised tools could ensure that decisions are made in an open, transparent manner that is immune to manipulation.

Corruption often thrives in systems where political power is concentrated in the hands of a few individuals. A decentralised, politician-free system could help to distribute power more evenly and make it harder for any one person or group to abuse the system for their benefit.

More Inclusive and Participatory Governance

Traditional political systems often exclude large segments of the population, particularly marginalised groups, from meaningful participation in governance. A politician-free future, powered by digital platforms and direct democracy, could allow for more inclusive decision-making processes where all citizens have a voice.

In such a system, people would no longer be passive recipients of government policies but active participants in shaping them. By enabling citizens to vote on policies directly or through delegated votes to experts, a politician-free system could empower people who have traditionally been excluded from the political process.

Efficiency and Evidence-Based Policy

In a politician-free system, decision-making could be driven by data, evidence, and expert analysis rather than political ideology or partisanship. AI and algorithmic governance could ensure that policies are based on empirical evidence and long-term outcomes rather than short-term political gain.

For example, an AI-driven system could analyse data on healthcare outcomes and recommend the most cost-effective interventions, or it could identify which infrastructure projects would have the greatest positive impact on the economy. This approach could lead to more efficient allocation of resources and better outcomes for citizens.

Elimination of Political Gridlock

Political gridlock has become a significant problem in many democracies, where partisan polarisation and legislative inefficiency have led to stagnation. A politician-free future could eliminate this gridlock by streamlining decision-making processes. Citizens could vote on policies directly, and AI algorithms could help identify consensus solutions that are in the public interest.

In a decentralised system, governance would be more agile and responsive to changing circumstances. Policies could be updated and refined in real-time based on new data and citizen input without the delays caused by partisan bickering or bureaucratic red tape.

Risks and Pitfalls of a Politician-Free Future

While the idea of a politician-free future offers exciting possibilities, it is not without its risks and pitfalls. Several challenges could emerge in the implementation of such a system, and these must be carefully considered before moving forward.

The Digital Divide and Inequality

One of the most significant risks of a politician-free system is the potential for exacerbating existing inequalities. In many parts of the world, access to digital technology and the Internet is uneven, creating a 'digital divide' that could leave some citizens unable to participate in governance. Wealthier urban populations are more likely to have access to the tools necessary for direct democracy and digital participation, while rural or low-income populations may be left behind.

Without careful attention to ensuring equal access to technology, a politician-free system could deepen existing disparities and marginalise already vulnerable communities.

Algorithmic Bias and Lack of Accountability

While AI and algorithms hold great promise for improving governance, they also come with significant risks. Algorithms are created by humans, and as such, they can be biased. AI systems may unintentionally reinforce existing social inequalities or make decisions that benefit certain groups over others.

Furthermore, the use of AI in governance raises questions about accountability. If an AI system makes a flawed decision, who is responsible? In traditional systems, politicians are accountable to the electorate, but in a politician-free system, it may be harder to determine who should be held accountable for decisions made by machines.

Case Study – Algorithmic Discrimination

There have already been several high-profile cases of algorithmic bias in areas such as criminal justice and hiring. For example, a widely used AI tool for predicting recidivism rates in the US justice system was found to disproportionately label Black defendants as high-risk. These types of biases could have serious consequences if they are allowed to influence public policy.

Populism and the Tyranny of the Majority

One of the dangers of direct democracy is the potential for populism and the 'tyranny of the majority'. In a system where citizens vote directly on every issue, there is a risk that the majority could impose its will on minority groups, leading to the erosion of rights and protections for vulnerable populations.

For example, referendums on controversial issues such as immigration, LGBTQ+ rights, or minority religious practices could result in policies that discriminate against certain groups. In a politician-free system, there would need to be strong safeguards to protect the rights of minorities and ensure that governance remains inclusive and equitable.

Loss of Expertise and Long-Term Vision

Politicians, for all their flaws, often rely on expert advisers and civil servants to make their decisions. In a politician-free future, there is a risk that the public may make decisions based on short-term concerns or misinformation rather than relying on the expertise of trained professionals.

Direct democracy can lead to impulsive decision-making driven by emotions rather than facts. For example, public opinion may be swayed by fear or misinformation during a crisis, leading to poor policy choices. Without the checks and balances provided by experienced politicians and expert advisers, governance could become more reactive and less strategic.

Hybrid Models and the Path Forward

Given the benefits and challenges of a politician-free future, the most realistic path forward may be a hybrid model that combines elements of direct democracy and technological governance with traditional political institutions. Rather than eliminating politicians altogether, this approach would aim to reform and enhance existing systems, making them more transparent, participatory, and responsive to citizen needs.

Liquid Democracy: A Middle Ground

One promising model is liquid democracy, which combines the best aspects of representative and direct democracy. In a liquid democracy, citizens can vote directly on policy issues or delegate their votes to trusted representatives who have expertise in specific areas. This model allows for more citizen participation while still benefiting from the knowledge and experience of experts.

Case Study – Liquid Feedback

Liquid Feedback is a digital platform used by Germany's Pirate Party that allows citizens to vote on policy proposals or delegate their votes to others. This system offers flexibility, enabling citizens to participate directly in issues they care about while relying on experts for more technical decisions.

AI-Assisted Governance with Human Oversight

Another potential solution is to use AI and algorithms to assist in governance while maintaining human oversight to ensure accountability and fairness. AI systems could analyse data and provide recommendations, but final decisions would still be made by elected officials or citizen assemblies. This approach leverages the strengths of technology while mitigating the risks of algorithmic bias and lack of accountability.

Case Study – Estonia's e-Governance

Estonia has become a global leader in e-governance, using digital tools to streamline government services and improve transparency. While the Estonian system still relies on elected officials, it demonstrates how technology can enhance governance without replacing politicians entirely.

Enhancing Transparency and Accountability

Regardless of the specific model chosen, any politician-free or hybrid system must prioritise transparency and accountability. Blockchain technology, for example, could be used to ensure that all decisions are recorded transparently and cannot be tampered with. AI systems must be designed with ethical considerations in mind, and their decision-making processes should be open to public scrutiny.

A Future Without Politicians?

The idea of a politician-free future is both intriguing and fraught with challenges. While technological advancements offer exciting possibilities for more transparent, efficient, and participatory governance, the risks of inequality, algorithmic bias, and populism must be carefully managed. A completely politician-free system may not be feasible or desirable, but a hybrid model that incorporates elements of direct democracy, AI, and decentralised decision-making could offer a path forward.

Ultimately, the future of governance will depend on finding a balance between technology and human oversight, decentralisation and expertise, and majority rule and minority rights. By embracing the possibilities of a politician-free future while remaining mindful of its pitfalls, societies may be able to create more democratic, responsive, and inclusive political systems for the twenty-first century and beyond.

CHAPTER 17

◆◆◆

Indian Democracy: Navigating the Maze of Politics and the Way Forward

India, a nation of unparalleled diversity and complexity, stands as a testament to the endurance of democracy amid chaos. Defying the scepticism of colonial rulers who doubted its ability to function as a unified nation, India has emerged as a vibrant laboratory of political experimentation. Interestingly, while this is true for India, the opposite is also true. Yet, as it strides into the twenty-first century, the world's largest democracy grapples with challenges that test the very foundations of its political system.

This chapter delves into the evolution of India's political parties, the intensifying polarisation, and the interplay of education and caste and proposes a way forward to enhance governance through increased citizen participation and reforms.

The evolution of political parties in India is a complex and multifaceted journey that mirrors the diverse and dynamic nature of the country's political landscape. Here's a broad overview of the key phases and developments in the evolution of political parties in India.

Pre-Independence Era: The Seeds of Political Consciousness

Before 1947, India's political landscape was dominated by the Indian National Congress (INC), which spearheaded the freedom movement against British colonial rule. The INC was not just a party but a broad coalition representing diverse interests unified by the goal of independence. Alongside, the All-India Muslim League (AIML) emerged, advocating for Muslim interests and eventually leading to the demand for Pakistan. This period laid the groundwork for political mobilisation based on ideology, religion, and communal identities.

Post-Independence Consolidation: One-Party Dominance

Following independence, the INC continued its dominance under leaders like Jawaharlal Nehru, Sardar Patel, and later Indira Gandhi. The early years were marked by efforts to consolidate the political system and the nation, address the partition's aftermath, and set the course for economic development. Despite India's diversity, a one-party system prevailed, though regional parties began to gain traction, reflecting linguistic and cultural identities.

The Era of Coalition Politics: Fragmentation and Alliances

The 1970s and 1980s saw cracks in the INC's dominance. The Emergency period (1975–1977) eroded public trust, leading to the rise of the Janata Party, a coalition of opposition groups. However, internal discord led to its downfall, and the INC returned to power. Regional parties like the Dravida Munnetra Kazhagam (DMK) in Tamil Nadu and the Telugu Desam Party (TDP) in Andhra Pradesh started asserting themselves, highlighting regional aspirations and contributing to a more fragmented political landscape.

Mandal and Mandir Politics: Identity-Based Mobilisation

The late 1980s and early 1990s were transformative, marked by the implementation of the Mandal Commission's recommendations for reservations for Other Backward Classes (OBCs). This move polarised society along caste lines. Simultaneously, the Ram Janmabhoomi movement, advocating the construction of a temple at a disputed site in Ayodhya, brought religious nationalism to the fore. The Bhartiya Janata Party (BJP) capitalised on these sentiments, propelling itself as a major political force with its Hindutva agenda.

Economic Reforms and the Rise of Regional Parties

The early 1990s ushered in economic liberalisation under Prime Minister P.V. Narasimha Rao and Finance Minister Manmohan Singh. While opening India's economy, this period also saw regional parties strengthening their positions. States like West Bengal, Tamil Nadu, and Uttar Pradesh became political arenas where regional parties held significant sway, often dictating terms in coalition governments at the centre.

Coalition Governments and a Multi-Party System

From the late 1990s onward, no single party could secure an absolute majority, leading to the era of coalition governments. The National Democratic Alliance (NDA), led by the BJP, and the United Progressive Alliance (UPA), led by the INC, became prominent coalitions. Regional parties became kingmakers, their support crucial for government formation, which added layers of complexity to policy-making and governance.

The Contemporary Landscape: Dominance and Challenges

In recent years, the BJP, under Prime Minister Narendra Modi, had secured decisive mandates in the 2014 and 2019 general elections and returned for the third time on a multi-party coalition-based majority after the 2024 elections, signalling a shift toward more centralised political power. However, the INC and various regional parties continue to influence the political discourse, especially in states with distinct linguistic and cultural identities.

New entrants like the Aam Aadmi Party (AAP) have disrupted traditional politics, particularly at the state level, emphasising issues like anti-corruption and governance reforms. It's essential to note that the political scenario in India is dynamic, and changes are the norm. Additionally, local and state-level politics often shape the overall political landscape, with alliances and realignments occurring based on regional dynamics and issues and political expediency rather than ideologies. The fortunes of political parties ebb and flow, as we have seen in the case of Congress and the Bahujan Samajwadi Party. The latter, once a dominant ruling party in UP, is now a non-entity.

Political Polarisation: A Deepening Divide Manifestations of Polarisation

Political polarisation in India manifests when parties and their supporters gravitate toward ideological extremes, impeding consensus-building. This divide hampers legislative processes, leading to gridlocks in parliament and state legislatures. Critical issues like economic reforms, social justice, and national security often become arenas for partisan battles rather than collaborative policy-making. The implications of this polarisation are profound, affecting the very fabric of governance.

Political Parties Today: Navigating the Maze of Polarisation

Several factors contribute to this polarisation.

Economic Inequality: Widening economic disparities fuel tensions. The affluent, wielding significant political influence, may resist reforms that threaten their interests, while the marginalised struggle to have their voices heard.

Identity Politics: Caste, religion, and regional identities have long been mobilisation tools in Indian politics. Parties often exploit these identities to consolidate vote banks, deepening societal divisions and contributing to an 'us versus them' mentality.

Media and Social Media Influence: The proliferation of media outlets and social media platforms has amplified partisan messaging. Echo chambers reinforce existing beliefs, and misinformation can spread rapidly, exacerbating divisions. Online spaces become battlegrounds where political adversaries engage in verbal duels, further deepening the schisms.

Coalition Politics: Inherent in India's multi-party system, coalition politics add another layer to the polarisation narrative. While coalitions are often a necessity for forming governments, the alliances can be tenuous, with parties compromising on their ideologies for the sake of political expediency. This can lead to shifts in political allegiances that contribute to a fragmented political landscape.

Interestingly, the messages disseminated by political parties play a pivotal role in exacerbating political polarisation. Despite a shared concern about societal issues and potential solutions, political polarisation takes root when politicians frame these matters through the lens of partisan politics. According to political scientists Gadarian and Albertson, this framing catalyses a polarisation of positions, transforming shared concerns into fiercely contested battlegrounds.

The connection between political polarisation and economic inequality unveils a complex interplay of power dynamics. Those in positions of influence seek to preserve their advantages, contributing to an environment where compromise becomes increasingly elusive. The consequence is a political landscape fraught with tension and division, where issues that could otherwise unite the populace become casualties of the polarisation dance.

Navigating the intricate choreography of Indian politics amid the spectre of polarisation requires a nuanced understanding of its drivers and consequences. The challenge lies in finding pathways to rekindle collaboration and bridge the ideological gaps that threaten the very foundation of effective governance. As the dance continues, the quest for a harmonious political landscape remains a crucial pursuit for the nation's collective well-being. The polarisation has left a trail of challenges, hindering the legislative process and obstructing the formulation of effective policies. As parties drift apart, the ability to find common ground diminishes, leaving critical issues unaddressed.

Impact on Governance

Legislative Paralysis: The inability to reach consensus stalls important legislation, hindering progress on pressing issues like healthcare, education, and infrastructure.

Erosion of Democratic Norms: Personal attacks and vitriolic discourse undermine the decorum of democratic institutions and erode public trust.

Policy Inconsistency: Frequent changes in government or policy reversals due to ideological shifts create uncertainty, affecting economic stability and investor confidence.

The Dynamics of Political Parties and Polarisation in India

Political polarisation in India manifests in the widening gap between ideological extremes, making consensus on public policy issues increasingly elusive. The diverse array of political parties, once emblematic of India's pluralistic ethos, now grapple with deep-seated ideological divisions that permeate various facets of governance.

Moreover, the role of leadership within political parties is instrumental in shaping the polarisation narrative. Charismatic leaders who command unwavering loyalty can cultivate a personality-driven politics that transcends party ideologies. This personalised approach to politics can create a polarising effect, with supporters rallying around a leader rather than a set of principles.

The impact of political polarisation is felt keenly in legislative bodies, where the ability to forge consensus on crucial policy matters becomes increasingly challenging. Instances of legislative gridlock, akin to those observed in other democracies experiencing polarisation, hinder the efficient functioning of the democratic machinery.

In the realm of elections, political polarisation influences campaign strategies, with parties often resorting to divisive rhetoric to galvanise their base. The emphasis on 'othering' opponents rather than engaging in substantive policy debates contributes to a charged political atmosphere.

As India navigates the intricate interplay of political parties and polarisation, the challenge lies in striking a balance between healthy political competition and fostering national unity. The diversity that has long been India's strength should be harnessed as a source of resilience rather than a cause for division.

In the quest for a robust and inclusive democracy, understanding the nuances of political polarisation becomes imperative. As citizens engage with the democratic process, they play a pivotal role in shaping the narrative, steering the course toward a future where political differences are avenues for constructive dialogue rather than fault lines of division.

Education, Caste, and the Kaleidoscope of Indian Politics

In the diverse tapestry of Indian politics, the interplay of education and caste dynamics has emerged as a pivotal force shaping electoral landscapes. As the country experiences socio-political transformations, the relationships between educational levels, caste affiliations, and political allegiances are undergoing nuanced shifts, defining the contours of India's democratic journey.

Education, once a subdued undertone in Indian electoral dynamics, is now asserting itself as a defining factor in political preferences. The correlation between educational attainment and voting patterns is evolving, and the twenty-first century has witnessed a notable rise in the political influence of educated voters.

In recent elections, urban and educated voters have shown a growing inclination towards parties that align with their aspirations for development, good governance, and economic progress. The traditional stronghold of rural and less-educated segments, often associated with regional and identity-based parties, is facing challenges from a new breed of voters who prioritise education as a catalyst for social and economic mobility.

Caste, deeply ingrained in the Indian social fabric, continues to play a pivotal role in shaping political affiliations. Traditionally, political parties in India have mobilised support along caste lines, leveraging community identities to consolidate votes. However, the twenty-first century has witnessed a shift where voters, particularly among the younger generation, are increasingly looking beyond caste considerations.

While caste-based politics remains a significant force in certain regions, there is a discernible trend of voters prioritising issues such as economic development, job opportunities, and social welfare over narrow caste loyalties. This evolving mindset is reshaping the political calculus and challenging the traditional equations that governed Indian politics for decades.

The emergence of educated and aspirational youth as a potent political force is reshaping party narratives. Parties are compelled to address issues that resonate with this demographic, pushing agendas centred around education, employment, and economic growth to the forefront. In this changing landscape, political parties that fail to adapt risk losing traction among an increasingly discerning electorate.

However, the transformation is not uniform across the vast and diverse Indian landscape. In some states, caste-based politics remains deeply entrenched, with parties continuing to rely on traditional vote banks. The coexistence of these contrasting trends underscores the complex and multifaceted nature of Indian politics.

As India grapples with these shifts, it faces critical questions about the role of education and caste in shaping the democratic discourse. The challenge for political parties is to strike a delicate balance, acknowledging the evolving aspirations of the educated and aspirational segments while respecting the socio-cultural fabric that defines the caste landscape.

In this kaleidoscope of Indian politics, where old and new forces converge, the democratic journey continues to unfold. The electorate's expectations, aspirations, and demands are redefining the contours of political representation, presenting both challenges and opportunities for a nation navigating the complexities of its democratic evolution.

Should Voters Join a Political Party?

In 2024, the BJP launched a drive to recruit new members in its cadre. The decision to join a political party is a nuanced one, influenced by a variety of factors, and it carries different implications in various world democratic systems, including India. Here are considerations for voters contemplating party membership.

The Pros

Active Participation: Joining a political party provides a platform for direct engagement in the democratic process. Party members at certain levels of seniority and positions have the opportunity to participate in decision-making, policy formulation, and party activities. However, most political parties tend to develop a centralised structure, a kind of self-serving oligarchy tightly controlling the affairs. The party workers and lower-level functionaries are unlikely to have much say in party decision-making as things stand today.

Influence on Policies: Party members can play a role in shaping the party's agenda and policies. By actively participating in internal discussions, individuals can contribute to the party's direction on issues they care about.

Networking Opportunities: Political parties offer a network of like-minded individuals who share similar political ideologies. Joining a party provides an avenue for networking and building connections within the political sphere.

Access to Information: Party members may have access to information about political processes, candidates, and policy initiatives before the general public. This insider knowledge can be valuable for making informed decisions.

The Cons

Loss of Independence: Joining a political party may require members to align with the party's official stance on various issues. This could limit the freedom to express independent opinions or divergent views. The party whip in directing its members to vote in a particular manner is an example of this loss of personal freedom.

Internal Politics: Like any organisation, political parties have internal politics. Navigating party dynamics and power struggles can be challenging, and individuals may find themselves in situations where personal beliefs clash with party priorities.

Party Loyalty vs. Public Interest: There might be instances where party loyalty conflicts with what an individual perceives as the broader public interest. Balancing allegiance to the party with a commitment to the greater good can be a moral dilemma. Switching of parties by individual members is sometimes a reflection of this dilemma.

Stigmatisation: In some cases, being associated with a particular political party can lead to stigmatisation or biases from those who do not share similar political views. This can impact personal and professional relationships.

Some of the considerations specific to India are:

Diverse Political Landscape: India boasts a diverse political landscape with numerous parties representing various ideologies and interests. Political parties often form alliances with parties with conflicting ideologies for political expediency. Voters should carefully choose a party aligned with their values.

Role of Regional Parties: In many Indian states, regional parties play a significant role. Depending on the state, joining a regional party might offer more direct influence on local issues.

Issue-Based Activism: In addition to party membership, individuals can engage in issue-based activism and social movements. This allows them to champion specific causes without necessarily aligning with a particular party.

Changing Political Dynamics: Indian politics has seen evolving dynamics, and new parties often emerge. Voters may choose to remain independent and evaluate different options as the political landscape evolves.

Ultimately, the decision to join a political party should align with an individual's values, beliefs, and vision for societal progress. Whether in India or elsewhere, voters should weigh the pros and cons, considering both personal aspirations and the broader implications for the democratic process.

In the digital age, where the virtual realm is as consequential as the physical, political parties are rewriting their playbook. The advent of the Internet and social media has ushered in a new frontier for political engagement. Acknowledging this transformative terrain, parties are amplifying their digital presence, leveraging platforms to connect with a broader audience. This strategic pivot, particularly targeted at the youth demographic, underscores parties' adaptability to harness emerging technologies for political outreach.

The traditional barriers posed by electoral systems, often accused of favouring established parties, have not stifled the potential impact of new entrants. The mere presence of a new party on the political stage can act as a catalyst, compelling established players to adapt their positions and policies in response to emerging challenges. The AAP in India has been the X factor, having won elections in Delhi for three consecutive terms against two powerhouses of the BJP and the Congress, yet consistently performing poorly in general elections to the parliament.

Crucially, the adaptability of political parties extends beyond electoral strategies. It encompasses a nuanced understanding of societal shifts, attitudinal changes, and the pulse of public sentiment. Parties that grasp these intricacies can navigate the complex labyrinth of contemporary politics with dexterity, ensuring their relevance in shaping governance and policy. Once seen as being on the road to extinction, the Congress party bounced back after the 2024 general elections and can be seen in the parliament with renewed confidence. Paradoxically, much against the expectation, they performed poorly in the Haryana State Assembly elections.

In conclusion, the saga of political parties is not one of inevitable decline but a testament to their evolutionary prowess. Far from being consigned to obsolescence, parties continue to recalibrate, innovate, and assert their relevance in the dynamic theatre of democracy. As long as the political landscape remains a mosaic of change, political parties, with their chameleon-like adaptability, are poised to remain indispensable actors in the democratic narrative.

> *'When a stupid government is elected in a democratic country or a state, the best thing about this is that you learn the number of stupid people in that country or state!'*
>
> —*Anonymous*

The Way Ahead: Implementing Direct Democracy

No form of governance is ever perfect. The Indian democracy, uncomfortably vibrant, is far from it. Governance is a living thing and dynamic. It needs to transform and evolve with changing times to respond to the needs of the people and the challenges of the times. One example is that while one needs an education qualification to be a peon, one needs no qualification to be a politician, an MP, an MLA, or a minister. These challenges make the Indian political system an interesting study for transformation.

> *'Our constitution has provisions in it which appear to some to be objectionable from one point or another. If the people who are elected are capable men of character and integrity, they would be able to make the best even of a deceptive constitution.'*
>
> —*Dr Rajender Prasad*

In the same vein, Dr Rajagopalachari had said, 'Take care of character, the rest will take care of itself… not this ism or that ism.' Are we electing men of character and integrity in Indian politics? When the answer is not an emphatic YES, then it is time for reflection and action.

In the preceding chapters, we have seen politics from multiple perspectives. We have also seen how countries across the world have adopted various practices of direct democracy to suit their requirements. In this chapter, we will make specific recommendations regarding implementing direct democracy in the Indian context.

Before we do so, it is important to reiterate the major challenges that face India. Broadly, these are as follows:

Size and Diversity: India's geographical spread, vast population, and diversity make nationwide consensus difficult. The complexity also does not allow a one-size-fits-all solution to most issues.

Digital Divide: Limited Internet access and digital literacy restrict the exploitation of the full potential of technology in the exercise of direct democracy.

Federal Structure: Balancing central and state powers complicates nationwide initiatives.

Social fabric and stratification need flexibility and adaptability for different regions, cultures, and sections of society.

Implementing direct democracy in India will require careful consideration of cultural, social, and political factors. It is important to strike a balance between direct participation and inclusivity and the need for expertise in policymaking. It may also involve constitutional amendments and changes to existing legal frameworks. Public support and awareness are critical for the success of such initiatives.

Implementing direct democracy, where citizens directly participate in decision-making, in a large and diverse country like India can be challenging. However, some mechanisms and practices can promote greater people participation in decision-making processes without disrupting the democratic framework. These are:

Mechanisms to Enhance Participation Referendums

Government-Initiated Referendums: The government can seek public approval on significant decisions, ensuring policies reflect the people's will. However, it's crucial to carefully select the issues that are suitable for referendums and ensure that citizens are well-informed.

Citizen-Initiated Referendums: Citizens can demand referendums on crucial issues, compelling the government to address public concerns. Case in point: the demand for a strong Lokpal (ombudsman) to combat corruption in public offices led to widespread protests because of the government's reluctance to introduce the well-intended proposal. A referendum could have expedited legislation reflecting public sentiment. Legislative proposals should allow citizens to propose laws if they gather sufficient support, ensuring grassroots issues reach legislative bodies. It is important to mention that the Lokpal and Lokayukta Act, 2013, seeks to establish a Lokayukta for states to inquire into allegations of corruption against public functionaries and related matters. It is an anti-corruption authority or ombudsman. Justice Santosh Hegde was the Lokayukta of Karnataka state in 2011. His investigation of illegal mining led to one of the three chief ministers he had named being sent to jail. Recently, in an interview with the *Indian Express*, on the level of commitment of various political parties to fighting corruption with institutions like the Lokayukta, he said:

> *'The truth is that none of the political parties wants this institution to function effectively, but the fact is that none of them also has the*

> *courage to abolish it. They are trying to denude the institution of its powers so that it loses credibility. Fighting corruption is only a slogan for political parties.*
>
> *In 2011, when we submitted the report on illegal mining… it was not implemented by the ruling BJP…. At the time, the Congress marched from Bengaluru to Ballari, saying the Lokayukta report should be implemented. They came to power in 2013 on this plank of illegal mining but did not implement the report…. On the contrary, they took away the powers of the Lokayukta….'*

Source: https://indianexpress.com/profile/author/johnson-t-a/

Corruption Among Politicians

The Prime Minister acknowledged corruption as a major issue from the ramparts of the Red Fort on Independence Day. Before the General Elections 2024, many MPs who were under the scanner for corruption from other parties jumped the fence to join the ruling party to avoid the corruption investigation. They were happily accepted. A senior minister, when questioned on this, replied that nothing has been proved; they are only allegations!

"I don't take bribes—it's more of a political action fee."

This only highlights the duplicity and yawning gap between political rhetoric and reality across parties.

In the vibrant democratic tapestry of India, public referendums represent a potent tool for direct democracy, especially on issues that routinely escape the political agenda of major parties. Unlike Western democracies, where referendums are more common, India seldom uses this democratic instrument. This rarity becomes particularly conspicuous when contentious or politically risky topics surface—topics that parties might sidestep due to ideological divides, electoral calculations, or fear of accountability, such as political funding.

Public referendums can rejuvenate the democratic process by placing power directly in the hands of the electorate, thus bypassing political gatekeepers who may resist changes that could destabilise their entrenched positions. For instance, issues like electoral reforms, the right to recall elected representatives, police reforms, or even more complex subjects like environmental policies and land acquisition laws, which provoke divergent opinions within party lines, are ideal candidates for referendums.

Moreover, referendums could enhance the legitimacy of decisions on such critical matters, ensuring that the resultant policies have a broad-based acceptance, thus reducing political polarisation. They also prompt greater public engagement in the political process, encouraging a more informed electorate that feels directly responsible for legislative outcomes.

However, the path to integrating referendums into the Indian political framework is fraught with challenges. These include ensuring informed choices free from populist influences, logistical difficulties in a vast and diverse nation, and the risk of majoritarianism overshadowing minority rights. Nonetheless, the strategic use of referendums could be transformative, offering a more inclusive approach to governance where the voice of every citizen is not just heard but is instrumental in shaping the nation's future. There are solutions to these challenges, as we have enumerated ahead.

Rhetoric and Reality

The duplicity and façade of honesty have to be ripped off through referendums. The biggest beneficiaries of corruption and misgovernance are the politicians themselves, whose fortunes change overnight. In the 76th Independence Day speech on 15 August 2022, the prime minister acknowledged corruption as a major issue, yet more than 40 per cent of MPs, including those from the ruling party, have criminal records, highlighting a discrepancy between political rhetoric and reality.

The saga of the Wrestling Federation of India (WFI), where its President, a BJP political heavyweight, was accused of sexual harassment by women wrestlers, exposes the duplicity of the political parties for political expediency. The government was forced to take action after months of street protests by national celebrity wrestlers and the intervention of the Supreme Court. This episode also highlights the fallacy of democratic elections, where money and muscle power trump ethics and the need for public participation. The possibility of blowback of women's vote in the ensuing elections finally forced the government to act. All this is when the government champions the cause of women's rights and dignity.

Countless cases expose the hypocrisy of political parties, as we saw in the run-up to the 2024 general elections in India.

Several investigations for corruption against political heavyweights were initiated when the present ruling party came to power in 2014; sadly, a decade later, nothing is heard of them. One is left wondering about the seriousness of the intention.

Another glaring example is the excessive perks for lawmakers that the lawmakers approve for themselves unanimously, all paid for by a small percentage of taxpayers. MPs get a pension for life, even for one term of five years, while government servants get a pension when they serve for decades. Instances like multiple pensions for MPs/MLAs are a case in point. In Punjab, in one case, an MLA was drawing ten pensions for having been elected ten times. The public should have the provision to call for binding referendums in such cases. Well, what is brutally disturbing and exposes the character and intent of politicians is that in the state of UP, the income tax of legislators was paid by the government from the taxpayers' money for decades till it was recently discontinued by the chief minister of UP.

The public should have the provision to call for binding referendums in such cases.

Electoral Bonds and Political Financing

The controversy surrounding electoral bonds raises questions about transparency and fairness in political financing. The justifications forwarded by the government counsel that the public was not entitled to know the source of funding and the donor did not want his identity to be disclosed is an affront to the voters' sensibilities.

Duplicity of Political Parties

All major parties have exhibited hypocrisy by campaigning against corruption and failing to act decisively against it once elected. The repeated failures of political parties to seriously address corruption and misuse of power suggest a need for more direct public involvement in decision-making through referendums.

Regional Variability in Policy Impact

The varied impact of national policies like the Farmers' Bill across different regions underscores the need for localised referendums to address regional needs and perspectives better.

Subjects such as gender parity, electoral and police reforms, freebies and welfarism, triple talaq and polygamy, National Register of Citizens (NRC), political corruption, same-sex marriage, etc. highlight the necessity of referendums to break the political deadlock.

Given India's multifaceted diversity, some of these could be national referendums, some could be gender-based referendums, and some could be regional referendums as deemed necessary.

The multiple aspects of the mechanism of calling for referendums by the citizens need to be carefully debated and formalised.

Public Participation in Decision Making

For every important policy decision, there should be input from the public obtained as under:

Forum of Subject Matter Experts (SME)

This could be based on a digital platform for SMEs to express their opinions or a series of debates like town hall meetings at the district level and TV debates held in different regions of the country. For example, if there is a decision that has major financial implications like the free rations scheme for 80 crore people for five years, or the implementation of the Old Pension Scheme by states or other such subsidies with far-reaching financial implications, economic experts starting from graduates in economics and finance could express their critical view on such a decision. Similarly, amendments to criminal laws could be vetted by SMEs of serving and retired lawyers and judges. These could be based on suitably crafted questionnaires or detailed discussions and interactions.

General Public Forum

The general public should be able to submit their opinions on secure and accessible online platforms, participate in discussions, provide feedback on proposed policies, and even vote on specific issues. This can enhance inclusivity and reach a broader segment of the population.

Media Engagement

Media can play an active role in facilitating public discourse. Balanced reporting and informative discussions can help citizens form opinions and engage in the democratic process. In specific cases, the government can ask the media to hold debates with stakeholders on issues being considered for policy formulation by the government.

Passage of Bills

Strengthening parliamentary committees needs to be revitalised to ensure a thorough examination of legislation. These committees could even have civil society members of repute and qualification for bipartisan input.

Based on the inputs from the above, a policy is formulated, or a decision is taken. This will ensure inclusivity and red flag public concerns. A well-deliberated decision will have wider public acceptance and prevent the repeal of the bills, as happened in the case of the Farm Bills.

Town Hall Meetings and Public Consultations

Regular town hall meetings and public consultations at local and national levels should be organised, allowing citizens to interact directly with elected representatives, government officials, and policymakers, and exchange perspectives on important issues, share information, and gather public input.

At the level of districts and panchayats, regular town hall meetings, and public consultations will enable grassroots inputs on important policies affecting people. These meetings provide a platform for citizens to express their opinions, ask questions, and contribute to decision-making processes. Similarly, a digital forum for getting the views of the general public who wish to participate should be obtained. This will ensure inclusivity.

Citizen Juries

Citizen juries or assemblies can be formed to deliberate on specific issues. These juries can be randomly selected or composed of volunteers representing a diverse cross-section of society. Their recommendations can be considered in the decision-making process.

Decentralisation

Promote decentralisation of governance by empowering local bodies and communities. Local governments can be given more authority over certain decisions, allowing citizens to have a more direct impact on issues that affect their immediate surroundings. This is feasible at the district and village panchayat levels.

Education and Awareness

Invest in civic education programs to ensure that citizens are informed about governance processes, their rights, and the issues at hand. An educated and aware citizenry is better equipped to participate meaningfully in decision-making.

Participatory Budgeting

Participatory budgeting, where citizens have a direct say in how a portion of the budget is allocated, needs to be followed. This can be done at various levels, from local communities to larger administrative units.

Electoral Reforms

Consider reforms in the electoral system that allow for a more direct representation of the people's will. This might include exploring alternative voting systems or proportional representation and processes that bring ethics into politics.

The following aspects deserve public participation.

Electoral Reforms: A referendum needs to be conducted seeking public opinion on the following aspects.

Ethical Politics: The fault lines in Indian politics have been elucidated in great detail earlier. The most important aspect is ensuring that the right man is elected and crime and money power are reduced to the extent possible in elections. The following are recommended.

Criminal Record: It is not enough for an aspirant to declare criminal cases pending against him before an election. Given the empirical evidence over a prolonged period, their character and crimes are public knowledge. Known offenders with police records get elected to public offices. Criminals and gangsters from UP who were elected multiple times and defied the law because of political patronage have been shining examples for decades. Thus, the question is, what is more important: the individual rights of a criminal or the public good of millions and the interest of the country? Is it justifiable to allow such gangsters to be MPs or MLAs on the principle of 'innocent till proven guilty'?

Thus, we need to empower the ecosystem to investigate and dispose of cases of politicians and aspirants quickly. We believe the judiciary should formulate parameters and guidelines based on which undesirable candidates with registered criminal cases should be debarred from standing for elections till proven innocent. While the downside of this recommendation is appreciated, the benefits far outweigh the shortcomings in the national good. Individual rights can never override national well-being.

Education Qualification: As of today, there is no laid-down education qualification required to be an MP or MLA. When the constitution was adopted in 1950, the literacy rate of people over 14 years was three per cent in two-thirds of the states and below ten per cent in all of the states. Under these conditions, it was understandable not to have any educational qualification. Now, in 2023, the average literacy rate in India is 74.04 per cent. The highest literacy rate in Kerala is 93.91 per cent, and the lowest literacy rate in Bihar is 63.82 per cent. The literacy rate in rural India is 67.77 per cent, while in Urban India, it is 84.11 per cent.

This is the age of computer literacy, too. This incident will drive home the point. In November 2023, during the debate in the case of one MP allegedly accepting bribes for asking questions in parliament, another MP stated about his parliamentary ID and password, quote, 'Even I do not remember my password. My PA knows it.... I do not know how to operate a computer.' So, is it acceptable to have MPs who take pride in computer illiteracy in this age of a technology-driven world? (Source: Improper and Illegal, KJ Alphons, Indian Express, December 14, 2023.) Even an Ola driver handles technology better than this MP.

The justification of 1950 has been rendered irrelevant by vastly improved literacy across the country. This will make a major difference in the quality of political leadership and governance.

Having said this, we need to legislate minimum education qualifications for MPs to be graduates and for MLAs to be educated at least up to Class XII. For village panchayats, the education qualifications should be Class V to ensure that suitable people who have not had the opportunity for schooling are not left out of the grassroots-level governance.

Budgeting and Electoral Promises

During the last state elections in Delhi and Punjab, the AAP promised fiscally unsustainable and politically motivated freebies like free electricity. When they formed the government, they were seeking central government assistance to meet those promises. The elections held in Rajasthan, Chhattisgarh, Mizoram, Madhya Pradesh, and Telangana saw all parties deeply engaged in 'competitive welfarism', making fiscally irresponsible and unsustainable promises of freebies. The ruling party, which criticised these tactics earlier as '*revdis*', itself did the same. While the debate between what is a public good and freebies will be never-ending, these promises need to be examined holistically, i.e., how they are going to be funded, how they impact other developmental projects, and whether they empower people to be self-sustained or are simply populist for elections. While we boast of being the fifth largest economy, the Prime Minister announced the extension of free rations for 80 crore people for the next five years, a little before five state elections. Clearly, there is a dichotomy between the two.

Accountability Through Taxpayers' Forum

In India, about 7.4 crore people filed income tax in 2023, of which 5.16 crore people, or 70 per cent, had zero tax liability. This means that just 2.24 crore people paid income tax in 2022–23. This works out to about 1.6 per cent of the population.

Should the people who shoulder the burden of such irresponsible and populist measures not have a say on how their hard-earned money is being spent by the government?

The Supreme Court had held a series of hearings on a petition filed by the BJP leader Ashin Upadhyay to direct the Election Commission of India to bar and de-register political parties from receiving irrational freebies from public funds. The bench seemed to agree with the premise, intoning that 'freebies may create a situation wherein the state government cannot provide basic amenities due to a shortage of funds'. There are many more issues beyond this.

Election Manifesto Audit

The state finances are finite, and therefore, all expenses must be subjected to a comprehensive review of relevant trade-offs.

How does one do it? The broad concept is to conduct an 'Election Manifesto Audit'. All parties must submit their manifestos to the Election Commission, including freebies and promises that involve funds, along with a financial support plan. A non-governmental panel of all stakeholders' experts committee must audit their capacity to fund those promises without relying on central funding support or sacrificing the basic requirements of the people. Those promises or freebies that do not pass this audit must not be allowed to be included.

Passage of Bills

The legislature is responsible for passing bills as representatives of the people for the good of the people. Parliamentary committees in India play a crucial role in the functioning of the parliamentary system. These committees are smaller groups of MPs tasked with specific functions, such as examining bills, overseeing government departments, and investigating issues of public concern. Lately, we have seen less and less engagement of these committees in parliamentary functioning. The experience of the Lokpal Bill and the anti-corruption Anna Andolan are examples where the legislatures avoid passing bills that hold them accountable. The Farm Bill 2020, which had to be repealed after a year of mass protest by farmers, is a good example of why stakeholder participation and consensus building are necessary. It becomes more important when a single-party coalition has the majority to pass bills on its own.

The lawmakers have always passed bills to raise their own pay, perks, and remunerations without debate or a single abstention. This deserves vetting by a referendum by taxpayers' committees or SMEs.

Thus, there is a need to institute a mechanism where citizens can call such acts to account and public scrutiny.

Non-Partisan Voice in Parliament and State Assemblies – Sortition

Barring the nominated members of the Rajya Sabha, members of both houses of Parliament and state assemblies are elected through elections. While this methodology meets the need for people's representation, it has its downside too. The members of parliament and the state assemblies are strongly polarised on party, regional, or caste lines. They oppose for opposition's sake, devoid of personal conviction, thus converting what should be a purposeful debate into an acrimonious inter-party battle for optics, irrespective of the merit of the case. Also, as we have seen earlier, a large number of them lack the education needed to chart the destiny of the nation, thus relying on the bureaucracy, which has not quite earned a reputation that people would expect it to.

The study of political parties' behaviour in India substantiates this assessment. As stated earlier, in the run-up to elections, all sane sense is thrown to the winds, and all parties indulge in scathing diatribes and 'competitive welfarism', literally trying to buy their votes from a short-sighted and ill-informed public swayed by freebies. We have addressed this issue earlier.

What we are now suggesting is that ten per cent of members in Lok Sabha and state assemblies must be constituted from non-partisan, non-elected apolitical erudite, administrators, educationists, economists, sociologists, women groups, legal, foreign affairs experts, and industrialists of good repute. This is a derivative of the historic Greek practice of 'sortition' that we have talked about earlier.

This concept aims at injecting an apolitical element that debates and votes based on the merits of the issue, devoid of any other consideration, in the best interest of the country. Some of the suggested guidelines are:

A government website be created that lays down the desired qualifications and experiences for this assignment. They should include aspects such as criminal record, declaration of assets, source of income, subject matter expertise, career highlights and achievements, etc. Qualified volunteers who wish to contribute to ethical governance should register themselves to be part of this pool for selection.

Eminent citizens of repute could be invited to be part of this select group. These are people who have demonstrated an apolitical approach, selfless public service, and a good understanding of national governance.

They 'serve' in the parliament for one tenure of fixed duration with no post-tenure benefits of any kind. They receive no pay or perks except what is needed to meet their expenses for discharging their duties; in other words, it is a service they discharge because of their commitment and conviction to the cause.

This concept can be followed for state assemblies as well. The methodology of selection could be evolved to ensure it remains apolitical and non-partisan.

The critical question is how one selects or nominates these people and how one ensures their impartiality. All rules of conduct of business in the houses will apply to these members as well. If these members are found to be indulging in misuse of their position against the spirit of their duty or seeking favour or gratification from political parties or any other agency, they will be held accountable during and even after their term of duty in the house. In essence, we are talking of people who are prepared to serve the national cause for free because of their conviction.

India's democratic journey is marked by remarkable achievements and profound challenges. The interplay of politics, society, and governance continues to evolve in a complex dance of progress and setbacks. As the nation grapples with issues like polarisation, corruption, and the need for more effective representation, embracing mechanisms of direct democracy and implementing thoughtful reforms becomes imperative.Empowering citizens through referendums, enhancing public participation, ensuring accountability, and injecting non-partisan expertise into legislative bodies can rejuvenate India's democratic ethos. While these steps require careful deliberation and the overcoming of significant hurdles, they hold the promise of a more responsive, inclusive, and ethical governance system.In the words of Dr Rajendra Prasad, India's first president: 'If the people who are elected are capable men of character and integrity, they would be able to make the best even of a defective constitution.' One can expect resistance from the politicians to any change that threatens their turf and holds them accountable. That is the very reason that demands a transformative change. The path ahead demands collective will and concerted action to ensure that India's democracy not only survives but thrives, reflecting the aspirations of its diverse and dynamic populace.

> *'Honesty is an absolute prerequisite to efficient service to the public. Unless a man is honest, we have no right to keep him in public life. It matters not how brilliant his capacity.'*
>
> —*Theodore Roosevelt*

CHAPTER 18

Just for Gags: Take Them Lightly at Your Own Peril

Note: This chapter is a collation of satires and fun-filled stories written by unknown people on actual happenings in the political arena. We acknowledge their contribution. It is meant for gags, and no disrespect is intended to anyone.

It has been a wonderful journey writing this book. It is a serious subject that needs serious deliberation. We believe that all serious deliberations must end on a lighter note. And we are ending this book on a humorous note, with all the seriousness with which we have written this book. Let us walk through some hilarious incidents that show that politics is a rich tapestry of drama, comedy, and absurdity, and India may be competing for the crown of the undisputed champion in this comic absurdity. From the Fodder Scam to college cheating, the antics of politicians provide endless entertainment and a healthy dose of scepticism. In a country where politics is a daily soap opera, humour helps the populace cope with the chaos. After all, the great Indian political circus is the finest free entertainment on earth.

The Great Indian Political Circus

The Inimitable Lalu Prasad Yadav and the Fodder Fiasco

'Jab tak rahega samosa mein aloo, tab tak rahega Bihar mein Lalu.'

—*Lalu Yadav*

Once upon a time, in the vibrant state of Bihar, often described as *Bimaru State* (Sick State), which continues to remain at the bottom of the progress ladder, there was a man named Lalu Prasad Yadav, a politician with charisma as colourful as the local festivals, despite the white khadi pyjama and banyan that he liked to wear. Lalu was the Chief Minister and the leader of the people, or so he claimed. But beneath his jovial exterior lay a tale of bovine betrayal known as the *Chara Ghotala* or the Fodder Scam.

The Fodder Scam was an ingenious plan. The target was brilliantly selected: the revered *Gau mata*—the holy cows. They were speech-impaired from the human point of view and thus could not protest or give evidence in court, and they were never the object of hunger index research—overall, a safe bet. The government allocated funds for cattle fodder, but instead of feeding the cows, the money mysteriously ended up in the pockets of politicians and bureaucrats.

Under Lalu's watchful eye, the scam milked the state treasury of around ₹950 crore.

One day, as Lalu sat sipping his tea, the press broke the story. 'Lalu Steals from the Cows!' screamed the headlines. The image of Lalu being chased by a herd of angry cows was too tempting for cartoonists to resist. In response, Lalu held a press conference, flanked by a bewildered-looking cow. 'This is all a conspiracy!' he declared. 'Ask this cow, am I involved?' The cow, unimpressed, continued chewing cud.

Well, *kanoon ke haath lambe hote hain* (The law has a long reach). Lalu did find himself behind bars—a curse of the holy cow, we guess. Not trusting anyone in the battle of thrones, Lalu forklifted his wife from the kitchen and planted her on his, the chief minister's chair, as he sidestepped into the jail. Salute the Indian politics. Well, Lalu was made the Railway Minister when his trial was going on from 2004 to 2009, a full five years—equivalent to one tenure in the Parliament. Innocent till proven guilty, even if the whole world knows the truth. Well, India gave the world the concept of infinity, didn't it?

If you recollect, we had asked a serious question earlier, 'Why are these politicians dying to get elected that they are prepared to kill, even cows?' Did you say public service? Hard to swallow. Lalu answered without realising that he had let the cow out of the barn. He was made the Railway Minister in the 2004 UPA government. He expressed his reservations about being given this ministry. He said that the first time there is a train accident, he will be asked to resign! That meant the loss of the golden goose, perks, power, and pelf, and a lot more. He probably did not know that the great Lal Bahadur Shastri had resigned voluntarily as the Railway Minister when a train accident happened during his charge.

Did you ever notice that politicians always build a good hospital in the city where the main jail is located? It is a sign of foresight and vision. They know that if the long arm of the law finally gets to them, they need a hospital to avoid spending time in jail. Pain in the chest is a reliable excuse that is hard to disprove and too risky to ignore. The hospital is more comfortable and respectable, ensuring better company and home food.

The Railway Revival and the Rolling Chapatis

As the railway minister of the behemoth known for its delays and antiquated systems, Lalu seemingly transformed the railways into a profit-making venture. How did he do it? By introducing *kulhads* (clay cups) for tea and promoting regional cuisine on trains. He always projected himself as the *Maati ka Lal* (son of the soil). No wonder, then, that he took the railway commuters back to their roots—*kulhad.*

One fine day, Lalu decided to showcase his culinary vision by personally cooking chapatis on a moving train. With cameras rolling, he rolled up his sleeves and started making dough. Unfortunately, his chapatis ended up looking more like maps of uncharted territories than round, edible bread. Passengers, amused, watched as Lalu tried to flip a particularly rebellious chapati, only for it to land on a journalist's face. 'This is the taste of progress!' he declared. In a manner, it was Lalu who, despite his wit, unwittingly launched the 'stand-up comedy' show. His press conferences were class comedy shows with little substance.

The Bridge to Nowhere – Political Corruption and Collapsing Bridges

Fast forward. For Bihar, despite having been governed by majoritarian caste-based political parties for decades, progress and development were bridges too far for the general public.

We now delve into the fascinating world of Bihar's bridges, which have a shorter lifespan than a broiler chicken. As for political corruption, it is as common as paan and *gutka* shacks on every corner. Here, we explore the absurdity of collapsing bridges and the politicians who promise more of them with more enthusiasm, seeing a golden lining in the disaster. While these collapsed bridges stranded the people and sent the taxpayers' money down the torrent, they were bridges to the prosperity of many politicians and babus.

It all begins with a grand announcement. Picture a politician standing before a large crowd, beaming with pride as he unveils the plan for a new bridge. 'This bridge,' he would declare, 'will connect our great state and bring prosperity to all!' The (paid) crowd erupts in applause, imagining a gleaming structure that will withstand the test of time. Poor fellows don't realise that this bridge is destined to collapse faster than they can spell 'funding scam', assuming that they have been taught by non-quota teachers in government schools.

Construction begins with much fanfare. Workers and engineers are seen bustling around, laying the foundation with a mixture of a bit of concrete, abundant hope, and just a dash of incompetence. Inspectors visit the site under the shade of an umbrella held by a labourer who could collapse under the weight of the umbrella itself. Their inspections are more theatrical than thorough, involving more chai breaks than actual checking.

The politicians, of course, are ever-present, posing for photographs with shovels and hard hats. Their smiles are as sturdy as the materials being used—both prone to cracking under pressure.

After an unpredictable delay, the inauguration day arrives. Just to digress a bit, once former Prime Minister Manmohan Singh was inaugurating a small-size dam. Uncharacteristic of him, he stated that he was happy to inaugurate the dam, but if it had been built as it was planned, that day, they would have been celebrating its silver jubilee.

The bridge, now complete (or so it seems), is festooned with garlands and banners. The politicians arrive in a convoy of SUVs (sport utility vehicles), each more luxurious than the last. The Chief Minister cuts the ribbon with great flourish, and the crowd cheers as though witnessing the birth of a new era. Little do they know, this bridge has a secret—it's held together by little more than optimism and under-the-table deals. Just for the additional safety of the minister and the bridge itself, the public is not allowed on the bridge till the minister is gone beyond reach. Just in case…!

The First Monsoon

Come the first monsoon, rain pours down, and the river swells up. The bridge, unable to bear the weight of its own existence, collapses spectacularly with chunks of concrete plummeting into the water. The remains of the pillars seen after the water subsides remind me of the Roman ruins in Mesopotamia. '*Khandahar bayan karte hain kee kabhee yahan koi pull tha….*' (the ruins indicate that a bridge existed here).

BLAME THE OPPOSITION...

The news spreads faster than the collapse itself. Headlines scream, 'Bridge Falls, Millions Down the Drain!' Politicians scramble to save face, blaming everyone from the contractors to the weather and even the neighbouring state for releasing too much water. The ruling party's first effort is to see how it can blame the opposition.

In the aftermath starts the blame game that makes quarrelling children look more mature. The contractor blames substandard materials, the materials supplier blames the contractor, and the politicians blame each other with the fervour of a reality show.

Don't be surprised if some adventurous politician suggests that the bridge was sabotaged by 'anti-development forces', blaming them for politicising the issue. Meanwhile, the public watches in amused frustration, knowing full well that this is just another chapter in the never-ending saga of Bihar's infrastructural misadventures.

The final saviour is God. The nearest village, trusting no one, decides to appeal to God Almighty. They make a small mandir at both ends of the bridge, trusting God to help the bridge sustain its own weight. The prayers work till the next monsoon when the expectations cross God's pay grade, too. All call lines to God get jammed as too many people are dialling Him for too many bridges.

The Promise of Bringing the Culprit to Justice

Of course, no collapse is complete without the formation of an inquiry committee. This esteemed group of individuals is tasked with finding out what went wrong, though their primary qualification seems to be an ability to drag out proceedings endlessly till something involving the opposition could be unearthed, under the dust and din of which, the debris of the collapsed bridge and public anger could be buried and forgotten.

The committee meets, debates, and eventually releases a report that is as thick as it is inconclusive. It suggests more inspections, better materials, and, of course, more funding. The irony is lost on no one—the very cycle that led to the collapse is now being recommended as the solution.

Rebuilding the Bridge for the Public Good

Undeterred by the disaster, the politicians promise to rebuild the bridge—better, stronger, longer, and more collapse-resistant than ever before. Another round of contracts is awarded, and the cycle begins anew. The public, ever the optimists, hope this time will be different, though they wonder how long the new bridge will last. The 2024 monsoon saw 20 bridges come crashing down before you could say *Hamro Bihar*. The smart public of Bihar devised a new concept to enhance their chances of survival from collapsing bridges: reduce the time on the bridge by driving at breakneck speed. The police, ever so concerned for the well-being of people, gravitate to this killing area. They let them off with a pocketed fine of just ₹200 that goes straight into their deep pocket, rather than ₹1000 that should go to the government. This empathy for the common man has earned the police people's goodwill.

Overall, it is a well-oiled echo system in which everyone except Mother India thrives.

Well, the rebuilding promise is preceded by brilliant spin masters who try to convince the public that a collapsed bridge is not all that bad for the economy of the region. Here is how it goes:

The collapse of a bridge is not a sudden event. The shaky foundation of the bridge was laid during the elections when corrupt politicians were elected on some affiliation. Then follows the dubious tender process, which selects the L1 bidder. Before the bridge falls, so many have fallen down the path of corruption. The first in line is the administration. This has the politician as the master blaster, followed by accomplished babu—the bazballer who has mastered the art of reaping the benefits without getting caught, or rarely. The wicketkeepers are a clan of engineers, and there are many in this minority community. In some states, a 40 per cent commission was reportedly being sought on every infrastructure project by the elected representatives. Naturally, bridges built on air cushions will not sustain the first sneeze of the monsoon. Following their leadership by personal example are the ball boys on the boundary—every man in the chain who has a nuisance value collects his toll.

Seeing the great ethical opportunity, the contractor grabs it with both hands and converts concrete into gold. He must make hay while the sun shines before the next monsoon strikes. Well, why should the poor public be left behind in this free-for-all market economy? Our very user-friendly nation, where the public has gotten used to freebies—with free rations, train and bus rides, free electricity, etc., must come with free construction material from the bridge site to renovate their houses.

Well, when so many have fallen before it, the poor bridge has no locus standi to stand for too long. It must fall to rise again of its own weight.

Now, the spin masters are let loose on social media and blame the invisible hand of anti-development forces. A vague term that could include termites, the intrusive media, the opposition—if they have laid the foundation stone—and the ultimate—the foreign hand.

The ultimate spin doctor tried to convince the electorate of the benefits of a collapsed bridge. Here it goes:

'A collapsed bridge is not such bad news after all. When a bridge collapses, a new one will be built. It will generate employment, cement, sand, etc.; the steel industry will get more business. It will crank the regional economy. The politicians and the officials will make money, and they will buy land and houses. It will also come back to the economy, and that will help us to become the third-largest economy very soon. It will elevate our international image.'

So, Bihar, as their spin master would like you to believe, will be on the road (without bridges) to progress, having lost 12 bridges in 20 days, quite like nine pins. To solve this problem, the government of Bihar has decided to issue health cards to all the bridges for maintenance. It is like issuing health cards to the public when the healthcare system has eroded from within due to corruption and mismanagement. We have to wait and see how this overcomes the fatal cancer of corruption that has not changed.

In the end, the story of Bihar's bridges is a microcosm of political corruption and bureaucratic inefficiency. It's a tale where promises are as flimsy as their bridges, and collapses are as predictable as the monsoon rains. Yet, the wonderful people of Bihar remain resilient, finding humour in the absurdity and hope in the promise of a better future, held up by little more optimism and their belief in democracy, however, misplaced.

Unable to build bridges in their own land that can withstand their own weight, they pack their bags and head off to distant parts of the country where they build others' bridges, tunnels, and buildings that stand tall. What an irony!

So, here's to the bridges of Bihar—*may they one day stand tall and proud, and may the politicians who promise them learn to build them with integrity mixed with concrete, not just promises ambition.* Until then, we'll enjoy the free entertainment, shaking our heads at the grand spectacle that is Bihar's political drama.

(Source: Extrapolated from multiple sources)

Cheating Makes for Good Politics – Mulayam's Masterclass

A College Examination in Progress in UP

Politics and education have a curious relationship in the heartland of India, UP. Politicians, by and large, cannot boast of being well educated, degree notwithstanding. And no one exemplified this better than Mulayam Singh Yadav, the former Chief Minister of UP.

During a press conference about educational reforms, which included strict regulations against cheating in examinations, vide UP Anti-Copying Act, 1992 by the ruling BJP Government, Mulayam made a statement that would go down in history as both outrageous and oddly endearing to some. With a straight face, he said, 'If you stop students from cheating in exams, you will ruin their careers.' For a moment, the room was silent. Journalists blinked, unsure if they had heard correctly. Then, as the realisation dawned, the smirky laughter began. Later, as the Chief Minister of UP, he abolished the Anti-Copying Act.

(Source: https://www.indiatoday.in accessed on 18 April 2025)

What a visionary leader! He meant it. In recognition of his intellect and visionary vision, he was later appointed the Defence Minister of India. What a paradox: a value-based military headed by a minister who sees virtue in cheating.

The statement quickly became the talk of the town and the nation. Newspaper cartoons depicted students in examination halls, their desks piled high with textbooks, while invigilators looked the other way, all thanks to Mulayam's newfound education policy. Memes flooded social media, featuring Mulayam with captions like 'The Cheaters' Saviour' and 'Mulayam: The Patron Saint of Exam Tactics'.

Students, naturally, were thrilled. Overnight, Mulayam became a hero among the student community. In classrooms across UP, whispers of 'Mulayam Baba Ki Jai!' could be heard. Some enterprising students even printed T-shirts with Mulayam's face and the slogan, 'Cheat to Succeed'. For them, the Chief Minister had finally acknowledged the reality of their struggles—struggles against textbooks, long syllabi, and the dreaded final exams.

Mulayam Yadav's vision on cheating would not create professors or scientists, but it certainly created skilled mountaineers.

In 2023, the socialist leader was posthumously conferred with Padma Vibhushan, India's second-highest civilian award, by the Government of India.

Dissatisfied with this award, his Samajwadi Party, led by his son, demanded that his visionary father, who saw in cheating what no one else could, be honoured with Bharat Ratna! So, a Padma Vibhushan for a political leader who supported cheating in examinations.

Well, Mulayam may have had a vision that no one else could see, even with night-vision binoculars.

Ask a Bihari what is there to proud of about Bihar, and pat comes the reply. It is the state where the world-famous Nalanda

University existed in Bihar in the twelfth century. According to the National Statistical Office, Bihar ranks third from the bottom in literacy rate in India. In Bihar, the deputy chief minister's education qualification was Class IX. He could have done better if cheating were enshrined in the constitution as a fundamental right to career progression, going by Mulayam's logic. His boss, Nitish Kumar, an engineer by degree, matched his deputy in some ways, taking oath as chief minister nine times, changing alliances for political expediency to retain power, even with avowed political enemies.

Well, the political vultures are scouting for such a political no-ball to hit a six to deflect heat from themselves. Rival politicians seized the opportunity to poke fun at Mulayam. During a legislative assembly session, one opposition leader humorously suggested that a new university be established in Mulayam's honour—'The University of Cheatology'. Mulayam, never one to back down, retorted, 'At least my students will have degrees, unlike yours, who keep failing!' Grant him some sense of humour.

Well, if this is not bad enough, when some boys were involved in a brutal gangrape of a minor girl, he stated, 'These are boys; they make mistakes sometimes.' Wonder what he would have said if the victim were his daughter.

Well, if anyone ever deserved a Bharat Ratna, it was him!

The Midnight Horse Trading Drama – Check Your Ticket Before Boarding the Bus

Indian politics is famous for its unpredictability, and no event captures this 'tragicomedy' better than the midnight horse-trading dramas during elections. Particularly amusing yet unethical incidents take place during state assembly elections. Politicians are whisked away to luxury resorts in the remotest part of the country in strict secrecy, ostensibly to prevent 'poaching' by rival parties—such is the vulnerability and trustworthiness of our elected leaders.

In one instance, an entire bus full of MLAs was driven to a five-star beach resort under the cover of darkness. The operation was so secretive that one MLA, half-asleep, boarded the wrong bus and ended up at a rival party's resort. Upon arrival, he was welcomed with open arms and a fruit basket before awkwardly realising his mistake. By morning, he had become a viral meme, with captions like 'Resort Politics: Check Your Ticket Before Boarding!'

So, when you know that a full luxury resort has been booked by political parties in one part of a country, chances are that a government is under threat in the opposite part of the country—the breaking news is not far.

The Vote-for-Note – Why Kurta Pyjama is the Perfect Politician Dress

Indian elections are a spectacle in themselves, often compared to the grandest of festivals. However, behind the scenes, vote re-engineering is as common as bargaining in a fish market. The 'Vote-for-Note' scandal is a perfect example of this.

In 2008, during a crucial parliamentary vote, bundles of cash were openly exchanged for votes. The scandal came to light when a sting operation revealed MPs accepting bribes in exchange for supporting a confidence motion. The visuals of politicians stuffing their kurta pockets with wads of cash were broadcast nationwide, causing public outrage and providing fodder for late-night comedians. In one case, one defiant wad, a veteran of many pockets, refused to enter the overcrowded pocket and repeatedly kept falling to the floor. The 'Swachh Bharat' conscious politician would leave no paper trail behind, quickly picking up the bundle and wondering where to stuff them in full view of the camera. The defiant wad finally found the pride of place in his underwear. Well, mentally sharp as politicians are, they were never again embarrassed as the kurta pyjama pockets were redesigned to become deep, bottomless pockets to match their insatiable appetite for money.

They also designed a vest with pockets. I won't be surprised if someone tries patenting the fashion design!

Elections are a contest between the Election Commission of India and the political parties in note smuggling and its prevention. The vehicles get modified in all sorts of ways: false vehicle floors, divided fuel tanks in motorcycles, and all ingenious ways. Crores are spent on poaching rival candidates.

Spicing up Politics – Spraying from the Hips

You would have heard of masala chai, masala dosa, masala chips, etc. We thought Indian politics was hot enough in line with Indian cuisine. Sometimes, the state assemblies turn into wrestling arenas where 'might becomes right', and everything movable becomes misguided missiles. However, for some lawmakers, this is not enough; '*Yeh dil maange* more'. In an unprecedented and chaotic scene in the Indian Parliament, one MP from Andhra Pradesh, L. Rajagopal, not happy with the way things were proceeding, resorted to using pepper spray to disrupt proceedings during a debate on the creation of the new state of Telangana. As the MPs debated fiercely, nearly killing each other with their looks, Rajagopal whipped out a canister and sprayed it into the air, causing pandemonium. The first incident of chemical warfare in the temple of democracy, much against the UN Convention on Biological and Chemical Weapons.

In the next parliamentary debate, many MPs were seen armed with gas masks, given the ever-present threat of chemical warfare from frenemy colleagues.

The pepper spray incident became the butt of jokes nationwide. Memes quickly surfaced with captions like 'Spicing Up Politics' and 'Parliamentary Seasoning'. One popular cartoon depicted MPs wearing gas masks and carrying fire extinguishers, ready for the next session. The absurdity of the situation highlighted both the lengths to which politicians would go to make a point and the unpredictable nature of Indian politics.

Looking for spicy politics? Look no further. Fly to India.

The Election Season: The Great Indian Circus

Election season in India is like a month-long carnival. Campaigns are a mix of dance numbers, impromptu speeches, and promises that range from the realistic to the utterly fantastical. One candidate promised to bring the moon to his constituency. I think India could wind up the ISRO (Indian Space Research Organisation), which is wasting national money by going to the moon when some of our politicians can bring the moon to our doorstep. Who needs NASA (National Aeronautics and Space Administration) when you have Indian politicians, right?

And the campaign rallies? They're a spectacle in themselves. You have politicians arriving on elephants, camels, and even helicopters. It's like the circus came to town but with more slogans and more clowns. Some will come in wheelchairs, and others with a medical belt around the waist. They miraculously become fully fit the day votes are cast in their state. Like our politicians, these wheelchairs will surface again five years later.

It seems every party has a think tank dedicated to finding the meanest way of demeaning the opposing leaders and the parties. Some want to eradicate the Sanatan Dharma, equating it with diseases such as dengue and malaria. Some parties are scaring the hell out of people that the ruling party will change the constitution and stop reservations. The list is endless, and it only creates division within the communities. Nothing is contemptible in politics—everything is fair in the pursuit of power.

Well, this is not so bad after all. This story takes the cake. It was many years ago in Haryana, essentially an agrarian state, where a minister addressing an election rally said that the opposition party in the upper riparian state had extracted all the electricity from the water before releasing it to Haryana; that it would devastate agriculture in the state. Well, that minister did win the election by a big margin, after all!

And the election results? It's like the season finale of a cliffhanger TV series. Will the incumbent party retain power, or will there be a shocking twist? It's edge-of-the-seat entertainment, with news anchors playing the role of dramatic narrators. Well, post-2024 elections, many pundits went into hiding as all exit polls proved wrong. The winner claimed victory, as did the loser. The people showed who the master is.

The Post-Election Drama: The Never-Ending Soap Opera

Once the elections are over, the real drama begins—coalition formations. This is where politics turns into a soap opera with shifting alliances, backstabbing, and dramatic exits. One day, political rivals are at each other's throats; the next, they're shaking hands like long-lost friends, announcing an alliance. It's like watching a soap where every character is both the hero and the villain, depending on the scene.Well, India is a case of political discrimination in some ways. The most glaring is that a criminal locked up in jail for sedition can stand for elections and often wins, but the petty pickpocket cannot vote from jail. In the 2024 general elections, Amritpal Singh from Punjab, a self-acclaimed Khalistan activist, and Engineer Rashid from Kashmir, who has been in Tihar Jail for five years for supporting separatists, contested in the general elections and were elected as MPs.

If you ever feel down, just tune into Indian politics. It's the largest entertainment show on earth and is free. Who needs Netflix when you have news channels covering politicians arguing over who loves the farmers more while sitting in air-conditioned rooms? Lately, there has been a race to claim the legacy of Baba Saheb Ambedkar with an eye on the vote bank. India is the best place to be a journalist; you have breaking news twice a day, with anchors converting a debate into absurd theatrics. Ten people yelling at each other, sometimes ending in a physical brawl or one throwing water on another. At the end of an hour-long political debate, the audience is left wondering who said what. Every channel claims they are the most watched channel. While one channel thrives on noise, the other claims it provides news without noise. The problem with the media is that if you do not listen to the news channels, you remain ill-informed; if you listen to them, you remain misinformed.

And let's not forget the VIP (very important person) culture. Politicians block traffic with their motorcades so they can get to a meeting about reducing traffic congestion. The irony is so thick you could cut it with a knife. Have you heard of an MLA refusing to pay the toll and threatening the toll staff with a gun, ostensibly in self-defence, against a poor man armed with a pen in the booth? India has the largest number of VIPs in the world seeking all kinds of privileges.

So next time you feel the world is too depressing, just remember, somewhere in India, a politician is probably making a speech that will make you laugh, cry, and wonder, 'Did he really just say that?' Well, a politician in India is never wrong; he is always misquoted, and sometimes he misquotes himself. He is never at fault; it is always a political conspiracy.

Politics across the globe, by and large, fall into the same genre, barring some countries such as Singapore and some Nordic countries. The US is on the other extreme. We have seen the saga of the POTUS. Donald Trump, after two impeachments and a conviction on many counts of felony, has been elected the president for the second time, having dodged an assassin's bullet that clipped his ear.

The Bill Clinton-Monica Lewinsky episode exploded into the limelight some decades ago. Well, when dealing with the president, most people would bend backward, but Monica Lewinsky set a new trend when she bent forwards beyond the call of duty, and we are not hitting below the belt when we write this. Some presidents do work hard in the office, don't they? One wonders how the details of this top-secret liaison were revealed when no minutes of the meeting were recorded.

Well, Joe Biden thought that the spirit of the libido of the POTUS must not be allowed to die down, even if he was planning to quit the presidential race.

In the glittering ballroom of the White House, a gala was in full swing. Elegantly attired dignitaries, celebrities, and politicians mingled under the crystal chandeliers. It was an evening of splendour and class. President Joe Biden, ever the affable host, worked his way slowly to avoid tripping as he had once on the stage and thrice on the stairs of an aircraft, greeting guests with his signature charm.

As he approached a group of distinguished guests, he spotted a woman resembling his wife, Jill. Her blonde hair and elegant demeanour were unmistakable, and Joe's heart swelled with affection. Without a second thought, he moved in for a kiss, his eyes closed in anticipation of a loving reunion.

Just as his lips were about to make contact, the real Jill Biden appeared out of nowhere, her hand swiftly intercepting the misguided kiss. 'Whoa there, Joe!' she exclaimed, her eyes twinkling with amusement. 'I think you've got the wrong lady!'

The guests erupted in laughter as Joe blinked in surprise, finally realising his mistake. 'Well, I'll be darned,' he said, chuckling sheepishly. 'I must need new glasses!'

The woman who had almost been the recipient of the presidential smooch was laughing, too, her cheeks flushed. 'No harm done, Mr President,' she said with a smile. 'It's not every day I get mistaken for the First Lady!'

Jill, ever the gracious hostess, put a reassuring arm around her husband's shoulders. 'Come on, Joe. Let's get you a cup of coffee before you start proposing to the guests.'

The incident quickly became the highlight of the evening. However, the real buzz came the next morning when the media got wind of the near-kiss.

The headlines were nothing short of comedic gold:

- 'Close Call: Biden's Almost-Kiss Mix-Up at the White House Gala!'
- 'Biden's Blunder: How the First Lady Saved the Day!'
- 'The Kiss That Wasn't: Joe Biden's Gala Gaffe'

Late-night talk show hosts had a field day. Jimmy Fallon quipped, 'Looks like President Biden's kiss radar was a bit off last night. Good thing Dr Jill was there to save him from a diplomatic incident!'

Stephen Colbert couldn't resist joining in, 'Folks, it's official: President Biden needs GPS—Girlfriend Positioning System!'

The light-hearted incident brought a wave of humour to the news cycle, with pundits and comedians alike finding creative ways to retell the story. Social media was abuzz with memes and jokes, and even the White House press briefing saw a few chuckles.

Press Secretary Karine Jean-Pierre, with a twinkle in her eye, addressed the media frenzy, 'Well, I can confirm that President Biden knows exactly who his wife is. Sometimes, even presidents need a little reminder. And Dr Jill Biden is always there to provide it!'

In the end, the incident served as a delightful reminder of the humanity and humour that can be found even in the highest office of the land. And Joe Biden, ever the good sport, laughed along with the rest of the world, grateful for his wife's quick intervention and the laughter it brought.

So, here we are, two presidential candidates, one fighting a porn star hush money case and the other almost kissing another woman mistaking her to be his wife. Biden thought the misplaced kiss was because of bad glasses. Well, you can pardon him. The country needs a president who is farsighted politically; a wrong kiss is not such a disaster, is it? For sure, Americans had great choices for the POTUS. The world needed to be concerned. Well, the US has Donald J. Trump as the president again. The world is already squirming and in a huddle—the fun has just begun.

Well, with this humorous note, we bring this wonderful journey of writing this book on a subject of great significance to an end. We are certain this book will make you sit up and set you on an intellectual quest to find ways to improve governance by direct public participation, electing candidates on proven merit and character, and holding the elected representative accountable for non-performance.

Democracy is a government of the people, for the people, and by the people. Take charge; the future of the world is everybody's business.

Epilogue

◆◆◆

As stated earlier in the book, humanity has been at war for 93 per cent of its existence in recorded history. The world is facing grave security challenges in multiple hotspots across the globe; more than 68 countries are currently engaged in internal and external conflict, with many more sitting on a powder keg. The oldest democracy, the US, also the most powerful country in the world, has been at war for most of its existence, despite never being attacked on the mainland. Two major wars are raging as we write today, the Russia-Ukraine War and the Israel-Hamas-Iran War, that have impacted countries not even remotely connected with the wars. More than 1,62,000 people were killed in various wars in 2023. The political leaders of major countries involved have contributed to prolonging the war despite people's protests against it.

The bane of democracy is that people get to choose a candidate from those on the roll. The US elected a new president in 2024. They had two options for a president; one was a former president who created history by being impeached twice as the president and was engaged in all sorts of legal cases. He was generally considered an erratic president. The second, the incumbent, was considered too old with a fading memory, led a disastrous withdrawal from Afghanistan that left the country in ruins, leaving the country to the Taliban with a billion-dollar military equipment, which they had gone to destroy. He got his country involved in two major wars in a short span of two years, with no end in sight. Thankfully, Joe Biden pulled out of the race under pressure from his supporters, making a place for his vice president, who was party to his disastrous policies.

Should the elected few representatives have the liberty to engage in such misadventures against people's wishes?

The government machinery will have to be manned by someone; today, they are elected politicians who rank way down in the trust ladder across the globe. There has to be an arrangement for people to be represented and their voices heard. Should these people be elected from the list of self-serving with doubtful credentials, or selected/nominated from the most suited and qualified with proven credentials, or the ones that choose politics as a career who are filtered based on strict merit and integrity-based criteria and process? We have emphasised the need for a merit-based polity. A global scan of governments throws up just a few models that are worthy of emulation, and Singapore stands apart, where merit, ethics, character, and values are enforced and seen to be followed by their political leaders.

In a meticulous and highly scrutinous process stretching over four years, Singapore has set a new precedent in political leadership selection, finally deciding Lawrence Wong as its fourth Prime Minister. With a double postgraduate degree in Economics and Public Administration from Harvard, Wong's academic prowess is matched by his professional integrity and performance. Throughout the rigorous evaluation, he outshone other candidates by scoring highest in critical areas such as character, performance, integrity, quality, and key performance indicators. Remarkably, he scored zero in public complaints, traffic summons, racial hatred statements, corruption, bribery, legal court cases, tax fraud, abuse of power, and checks by the FBI, CIA (Central Intelligence Agency), and Interpol.

—Harsh Goenka

That is what we call a 'democratic delight'. Singapore places a strong emphasis on integrity and accountability among its political leaders. Elected officials are expected to uphold the highest ethical standards and are subject to strict codes of conduct.

The Singaporean politicians wear white to emphasise the need for integrity and clean politics. Great thought, indeed. Most politicians in India wear whites, too, but in most cases, the similarity ends there.

Compare this with other democracies. In India, for instance, there is no qualification to be a minister, MP, or MLA. Forty-three per cent of the MPs have criminal records, and dynastic politics is the order of the day. Caste-based politics trump merit and ethics.

Singapore's approach raises a compelling question for all countries. Could adopting such stringent criteria for political leadership elevate governance standards? Singapore stands as a beacon of excellence in all aspects of governance and public good, and it has to do with the quality of political leadership with a vision.

As India went to the polls in 2024, the political discourse reached its nadir. The unparliamentary conduct was overflowing both inside and outside the Parliament. Government enforcement agencies like the ED were accused of partisan conduct as elections approached. In 2024, seventeen serving and former chief ministers of states were under investigation for corruption. Is there smoke without fire? So much for political ethics. Some, under the scanner of the ED and under fear of landing in jail for corruption, jumped the political fence to join the safe havens of the ruling party. It was considered fair game—all is fair in war and politics. Some were even made ministers, and many were given party tickets for the general elections. So much for the clarion call against corruption that all governments make.

All this does not inspire confidence that political business must go on as usual in what is considered the best form of government. All organisations tend to turn into oligarchs. In a democracy, inclusivity and public participation are key. Examples across the world demonstrate that public participation is possible in different ways through different means.

Citizens are at the core of governance. No politician joins politics for public service, while there are only a few who could be remembered for leaving a legacy. Have we had another Lal Bahadur Shastri, who, as a minister, owned only one coat and took a loan of ₹6000 to buy a second-hand car? With all the technology at our disposal, it is time that politicians do not hold a monopoly on decision-making. The walls of dynasties and political and bureaucratic elitism need to crumble, paving the way for a more inclusive form of governance. Through innovative mechanisms such as direct public participation, citizens must become active participants in shaping policies that affect their lives. Town hall meetings, online forums, referendums, citizen assemblies, recalls, etc., have proven potential to become the new arenas where ideas must clash and consensus must emerge. We have seen many countries which have harnessed technology to enhance direct public participation and ensure government accountability.

Well, the greatest virtue of democracy is that people elect their representatives. The US, through a fair and legitimate election process, has elected Donald Trump for a second term. Trump 2.0 has shaken up the world with his personalised and transactional brand of politics that rewards personal loyalty over institutional expertise. His turnaround on internal and foreign policies has sent shock waves as the world looks at an uncertain future on all fronts.

Trump 2.0 is a perfect case study in the context of this book, which seeks to reduce the dangers of personalised politics and emphasises an institutional approach that holds politicians accountable while enhancing people's direct participation in policy formulation.

The quality of those who represent people has to undergo a profound shift. They need to be rigorously evaluated for their expertise, integrity, and commitment to public service through transparent selection processes and stringent accountability measures. People need to be represented by a new breed of leaders who prioritise the common good over personal gain and who possess the skills necessary to navigate the complexities of governance.

Well, can there be *politics without politicians*? The answer is that the need for inclusivity and representation of marginalised voices cannot be disregarded. Imagining a system of governance devoid of politicians does not look practical for the present, for various reasons. However, given the shortcomings of the prevailing system that we have analysed, there is a strong case to ensure a better quality of those elected to lead, enhance public participation in decision-making on issues that matter to them, and hold the elected representatives accountable in every respect. The measures that we have recommended provide the way forward for a better tomorrow.

No form of governance will ever reach perfection, for governance is a dynamic concept. It needs to continually evolve with changing times and challenges. We do hope that this idea of reimagining politics into politics without politicians will sow the seeds of exploration of de novo thoughts and debate that transform governance and, therefore, the lives of people and the future of the world.

More from The Browser

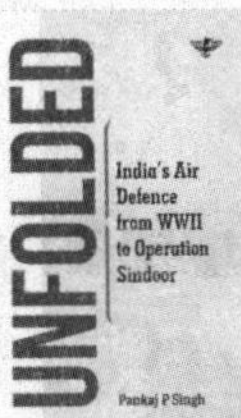

UNFOLDED: India's Air Defence from WWII to Operation Sindoor
Pankaj P Singh
ISBN: 978-93-49042-30-8

The Sacred Sound Path
P. Sesh Kumar
ISBN: 978-93-49042-84-1

Ability: Landmark Judgements on Disability Jurisprudence in India
Navdeep Singh and Shruti Bedi
ISBN: 978-93-49042-38-4

General's Jottings Rearmed: National Security, Conflicts and Strategies (Including Operation Sindoor)
Lt Gen KJ Singh
ISBN: 978-93-49042-24-7

Emergency and Neo-Emergency
M. G. Devasahayam
ISBN: 978-81-979897-5-9

Flowers on a Kargil Cliff
Vikram Jit Singh
ISBN: 978-81-979897-9-7

From Boots to Brotherhood
Shivam Sharma
ISBN: 978-93-49042-08-7

Catharsis
Mukul Kumar
ISBN: 978-93-92210-77-8

Ekarat: Stories He Left Behind
Ajay Khullar
ISBN: 978-93-92210-08-2

An Olympian's Tryst with Soldiering
Colonel Balbir Singh
ISBN: 978-93-92210-96-9

The Brown Goras of Brampton
Aparjeet Nakai
ISBN: 978-93-92210-40-2

Romancing the 50s
Harjap Singh Aujla
ISBN: 978-93-92210-80-8

Liminal Tides
Soumitra Banerji
ISBN: 978-93-92210-64-8

Dusk over the Mustard Fields
Ranjit Powar
ISBN: 978-93-88150-10-1

Black Horse Down & Other Stories
Ashok Ahlawat
ISBN: 978-93-92210-75-4

The Crossover Girl & Other Stories
Ashok Ahlawat
ISBN: 978-93-92210-22-8

For More Information